FROMMER'S
WALKING TOURS

LONDON

BY
DAN LEVINE
AND
RICHARD JONES

PRENTICE HALL TRAVEL

NEW YORK • LONDON • TORONTO • SYDNEY
TOKYO • SINGAPORE

FROMMER BOOKS

Published by Prentice Hall General Reference
A division of Simon & Schuster Inc.
15 Columbus Circle
New York, NY 10023

ISBN 0-671-79836-7
Library of Congress Catalog Card Number: 93-84074

Design by Robert Bull Design
Maps by Ortelius Design

FROMMER'S EDITORIAL STAFF
Editorial Director: Marilyn Wood
Editorial Manager/Senior Editor: Alice Fellows
Senior Editor: Lisa Renaud
Editors: Charlotte Allstrom, Thomas F. Hirsch, Peter Katucki, Sara Hinsey
    Raveret, Theodore Stavrou
Assistant Editors: Margaret Bowen, Christopher Hollander, Ian Wilker
Editorial Assistants: Gretchen Henderson, Bethany Jewett
Managing Editor: Leanne Coupe

Special Sales Bulk purchases (10+ copies) of Frommer's Travel Guides
are available to corporations at special discounts. The Special Sales
Department can produce custom editions to be used as premiums
and/or for sales promotion to suit individual needs. Existing editions
can be produced with custom cover imprints such as a corporate logo.
For more information write to: Special Sales, Prentice Hall Travel, 15
Columbus Circle, New York, New York 10023.

Manufactured in the United States of America

CONTENTS

LIST OF MAPS

SAFETY ADVISORY

Whenever you're traveling in an unfamiliar city or country, stay alert. Be aware of your immediate surroundings. Wear a moneybelt and keep a close eye on your possessions. Be particularly careful with cameras, purses, and wallets, all favorite targets of thieves and pickpockets.

INVITATION TO THE READERS

In researching this book, we have come across many wonderful sights, pubs, and restaurants, the best of which we have included here. We are sure that many of you will also discover appealing places as you explore London. Please don't keep them to yourself. Share your experiences, especially if you want to bring to our attention information that has changed since this book was researched. You can address your letters to:

Dan Levine and Richard Jones
Frommer's Walking Tours: London
Prentice Hall Travel
15 Columbus Circle
New York, NY 10023

Introducing London

By any measure, London is a very old city. Excavations show that there had been a settlement here as far back as 2500 B.C. Although scholars debate the origin of London's name, popular belief is that it comes from the Celtic "Llyn Din," meaning "lakeside fortress."

EARLY LONDON

When the Romans arrived in A.D. 43, they called the settlement on the Thames "Londinium." A bridge was built and the town began to flourish around the north bank of the bridgehead. In the latter part of the second century, the Romans built a massive wall of Kentish ragstone around the city to protect it from attack by surrounding tribes, and remnants of the wall can still be seen. Within a century the population had increased to 15,000 and Londinium became a bustling center of trade and industry. Roman Britain lasted until the end of the third century, at which time Saxon invaders began to encroach on southern England. Meanwhile, Rome itself came under siege, and in A.D. 410 London's Roman troops departed for home.

Over the next 400 years, various Germanic tribes, collectively called Anglo-Saxons, began to settle in England and by A.D. 871

were united under Alfred the Great, the first in the line of Saxon kings. He strengthened London's fortifications against the Vikings, whose raids were a constant threat. Edward the Confessor (1003–1066), who was later to be canonized, transferred the court and government from Winchester to Westminster. He rebuilt Westminster Abbey, and Harold II, the last of the Saxon rulers, was crowned there.

However, it was William the Conqueror who first understood the political importance of London and left an indelible mark on it. His coronation in Westminster Abbey in 1066 established a precedent that has been followed ever since. He recognized London as the capital city and allowed the City of London to continue electing its own leaders—a decision that was to have far-reaching consequences. English monarchs from that time on, eager for the support of the country's wealthiest people, strove to hold London as the key to controlling England. William also built the White Tower, which was later incorporated into the Tower of London.

By the 15th century the banks of the Thames were lined with warehouses and the great mansions of the merchants, the population had grown to 30,000, and ecclesiastical establishments whose names—Whitefriars, Blackfriars, Greyfriars—still remain a part of present-day London flourished. The suburbs expanded beyond the City walls and many new ones came into being; however, since there was no central planning, the roads developed haphazardly, creating the confusing street pattern that still exists today.

BEGINNING OF MODERN LONDON

Modern London began with the Tudors. Henry VIII built St. James's Palace and enclosed what is now Hyde Park and Green Park for his private grounds. But his Reformation and the dissolution of the monasteries brought about the destruction of many medieval ecclesiastical buildings—convents and priories were subdivided by narrow streets and courtyards and used for general housing. The wealth of the medieval church was confiscated and redistributed to a new aristocracy that supported the monarch; among those who were executed for refusing to acknowledge Henry's supremacy as head of the church was the internationally prominent man of letters, Sir Thomas More, author of *Utopia*.

The ascension of Queen Elizabeth I ushered in an era of peace and prosperity. Elizabethan England was a period of unparalleled creativity. Poetry, theater, and spectacle flourished. Open-air playhouses, including Shakespeare's Globe Theater, were built in the borough of Southwark (the city fathers had puritanically banned theaters in the belief that they attracted the wrong element). Plays by Shakespeare, Ben Jonson, and Christopher Marlowe were performed there. Along with the flowering of the arts, England had entered a period of colonial and mercantile expansion in rivalry with Spain, and London was a prime beneficiary.

All these trends continued after the defeat of the Spanish Armada and into the Jacobean period. John Webster's tragic dramas and John Donne's poetry continued literary and dramatic traditions. Inigo Jones (1573–1652), generally viewed as the first modern British architect, introduced Palladian style into London and built the Queen's House at Greenwich and the Banqueting House at Whitehall.

During this time the conflict between the Stuart kings and the Puritans steadily intensified, but religion was not the only issue. The king claimed the privileges of a divine-right monarch against a Parliament that advocated constitutional monarchy. After the Puritan victory in 1649, Charles I stepped through the window of the Banqueting Hall onto the scaffold and lost his head.

In the 10 years that followed, the arts were rigorously suppressed, and there was significant destruction to many of the important Gothic cathedrals—stained glass was smashed and religious artifacts destroyed. Although the great poet John Milton supported the Puritans, he published his most noted works, *Paradise Lost* and *Samson Agonistes,* after the restoration of Charles II in 1660.

Although plague had long been endemic in London, it did not rise to epidemic proportions until 1665, when some 100,000 Londoners—a fifth of the population—died. The Great Plague did not abate until a second catastrophe occurred in 1666—the Great Fire of London. Fanned by strong easterly winds, it burned more than 10,000 buildings and virtually destroyed the City of London, taking with it the crowded and unsanitary half-timbered buildings that had helped to spread the plague. After the fire, houses were rebuilt of stone and brick. Christopher Wren, who was commissioned to redesign the city, built his masterpieces: St. Paul's Cathedral and St. Mary-le-Bow, the Chelsea Royal Hospital, Kensington Palace, and dozens of other London buildings.

EIGHTEENTH-CENTURY LONDON

In the 18th century England was transformed into a world-class financial and military power, and London again became the primary beneficiary of the new prosperity. This was the great era of Georgian architecture, which can still be seen in Grosvenor, Bedford, and Hanover squares, as well as other London squares and streets. The

Georgian style spilled over into the applied arts, including furniture, silver, and glass. The great porcelain works and potteries of Wedgwood, Spode, and Staffordshire were established at this time. Two new bridges—Blackfriars and Westminster—were built, streets were upgraded, and hospitals were improved. A number of painters gained prominence, including Joshua Reynolds, Thomas Gainsborough, and William Hogarth; and several noteworthy sculptors (for example, Grinling Gibbons) emerged. Samuel Johnson compiled his famous Dictionary, James Boswell wrote his great biography of the lexicographer/critic, and David Garrick performed his memorable Shakespearean roles at his playhouse in Drury Lane (often changing Shakespeare's tragic endings to happy ones to suit the temper of the times). The newfound wealth of the Industrial Revolution led to the emergence of a middle class that was soon to partly merge with and bolster up the older land-owning aristocracy.

VICTORIAN LONDON

Queen Victoria ascended the throne in 1837 and reigned for 64 years—the longest tenure in English history. Since the new middle class believed learning was an integral part of prosperity, the University of London and free municipal public libraries were established. The National Gallery at Trafalgar Square was completed in 1838, while the British Museum's new building in Bloomsbury was finished in 1857. At this time progress changed the face of London, transforming it into a modern metropolis as rail lines and steam engines, underground trains, sewage systems, and new building techniques greatly expanded its borders. Buckingham Palace was enlarged and sheathed in honey-colored stone, and the Gothic extravagance of the Albert Memorial defined an architectural style that only recently has begun to be appreciated.

Victorian London was the center of the largest empire the world had ever seen. Londoners traveled all over the globe to fill military and administrative posts. This period is the one that still influences our present-day view of London and of the English: Victorian London, which was shaped by the growing power of the bourgeoisie, the queen's personal moral stance, and the perceived moral responsibilities of managing an empire. The racy London of the preceding three centuries moved underground. Meanwhile, in the poorer neighborhoods the dialects and attitudes (later referred to as "cockney") were developing. The cockney humor of London's vaudeville and music halls affected the entertainment industry from Sydney to San Francisco.

The shock of World War I marked the end of an era; it had been assumed that peace, progress, prosperity, empire, and, incidentally, social improvement would continue indefinitely. Following World War I came two decades of social unrest and political uncertainty, both at home and throughout the empire.

WORLD WAR II AND POSTWAR LONDON

During World War II London suffered repeated bombings and almost every notable building was seriously damaged. Trenches were dug in public parks, and the Underground stations doubled as bomb shelters. The heroism and stoicism with which this ordeal was endured is still a nostalgic memory to Londoners as well as a source of local pride.

Since the 12th century, the City of London has been governed by an independent corporation headed by the Lord Mayor. In 1986 central authority was replaced by a division of governing responsibility between the central government and the boroughs. Modern office structures, centrally heated apartment buildings, and successive waves of immigrants have literally and figuratively changed the face of contemporary London. Many tourists are disappointed when they first arrive because the past is not immediately or easily visible, but if they scratch the surface they'll find a complex city that is an amalgam of all the preceding eras. One of London's most colorful pageants—the Lord Mayor's Procession and Show—derives from the ancient right of the City of London corporation to require the monarch to ask the Lord Mayor's permission to enter the City's original square mile. The Changing of the Guard at Buckingham Palace and the Ceremony of the Keys at the Tower of London are other survivals, not to be missed.

Although many of the structures and institutions of the past are long gone, those eras are still reflected in street names. Bucklersbury and Lothbury refer to the "buhrs" or stone mansions of Norman barons. Ludgate, Aldgate, and Cripplegate are named for ancient gates of the city wall. The word "Barbican" derives from the watch tower that once stood in its place. In the Middle Ages "cheaps" were markets—hence, the origin of names like Eastcheap and Cheapside. Some streets bear the names of products formerly sold there; look for Milk Street, Bread Street, and Friday Street (where fish was sold).

London is one of the world's most exciting cities. Take advantage of its terrific offerings and unique opportunities. Explore the narrow alleyways of the City, enjoy lunch at a local pub, attend a free concert at a church, and strike up a conversation with the locals. Though you may need to speak first, you will generally find that Londoners are friendly and helpful. As you will discover, London is not a single, uniform city but a collection of towns, each with its own history and ambience.

The 12 tours in this book are organized by area or by topic. We have endeavored to take you off the main streets as much as possible; to lead you down unexpected passageways and into secluded courtyards; to introduce you to that most English of institutions, the pub; to guide you through the streets of Dickens's London and show you the landmarks he himself might still recognize; and to help you discover, all over the city, sites and corners you might not have found by yourself.

The approximate time each tour should take is specified. None of the walks is physically strenuous—each is designed to be accessible (and interesting) to all ages. Walk, look, listen, learn, and enjoy.

Getting to Know London

By any estimate, London is a grand city. Close to 7 million people, spread out over 600-plus square miles, perpetuate a dynamic urban growth that has been intensifying for centuries.

Despite its size, however, London is surprisingly user-friendly. The city's intricate public transportation network (one of the world's largest) seems tailor-made for tourists, from the clean Undergrounds and the fun double-decker buses to the famous big black taxis. In addition, visitor information services and tourist resources abound, helping to make your stay less complicated and more enjoyable.

GETTING THERE

BY PLANE

Several airlines fly the enormously popular routes from North America to Great Britain. Chief among them is **British Airways** (tel. toll free 800/247-9297), which offers flights (all but a few of which are nonstop) from a number of U.S. cities to London's Heathrow and Gatwick airports. It is the only non-U.S. carrier with its own terminal at New York's JFK, and probably the carrier with the greatest number of add-on options, which make a visit to Britain cheaper than you might have expected.

American Airlines (tel. toll free 800/624-6262) offers daily flights to London's Heathrow from five U.S. gateways—New York's JFK, Chicago, Dallas/Fort Worth, Los Angeles, and Miami.

TWA (tel. toll free 800/221-2000), which expected to emerge from the protection of Chapter 11 bankruptcy proceedings in 1993, offers daily nonstop flights from St. Louis to London's Gatwick airport.

Delta (tel. toll free 800/241-4141) offers daily nonstop flights from Atlanta, Miami, Cincinnati, and Detroit to Gatwick airport.

Continental Airlines (tel. toll free 800/231-0856) has daily nonstop flights from Houston and Newark to Gatwick.

Northwest Airlines (tel. toll free 800/225-2525) flies nonstop from both Minneapolis and Boston to Gatwick, with connections from Detroit to Gatwick through its hub in Boston.

United Airlines (tel. toll free 800/538-2929) flies nonstop to London's Heathrow twice daily from New York's JFK, and once daily nonstop from Newark, New Jersey, San Francisco, Washington D.C.'s Dulles Airport, Seattle, and Los Angeles.

Air Canada (tel. toll free 800/776-3000) flies to London's Heathrow nonstop from both Calgary and Edmonton three to seven times a week, depending on the season. From both Toronto and Montréal, the airline flies to Heathrow nonstop every day of the week. From Vancouver, daily flights either transfer through Toronto or (once a week) fly to London nonstop.

Virgin Atlantic Airways (tel. toll free 800/862-8621) flies to London's Gatwick from Newark, Boston, Miami, and Orlando, and to London's Heathrow from Los Angeles and New York's JFK.

BEST-VALUE FARES

APEX Generally, your cheapest option on a regular airline is to book an APEX fare. **British Airways,** for example, offers three types of APEX fares. The least expensive is a nonrefundable ticket that requires a 30-day advance purchase, and a stayover of 7 to 21 days. Passengers who prefer to fly "midweek" (Monday through Thursday) pay less than those who fly in either direction on a weekend (Friday, Saturday, or Sunday).

BUCKET SHOPS [CONSOLIDATORS] In its purest sense, a bucket shop acts as a clearinghouse for blocks of tickets that airlines discount and consign during normally slow periods of air travel.

Tickets are sometimes—but not always—priced at around 20%

to 35% less than the full fare. Terms of payment vary—say, anywhere from 45 days prior to departure to last-minute sales offered in a final attempt by an airline to fill a disturbingly empty craft. Tickets can be purchased through regular travel agents, who may mark up the ticket 8% to 12%, thereby greatly reducing your discount. Use of such a ticket doesn't qualify you for an advance seat assignment, and thus you are likely to be assigned a "poor seat" on the plane at the last minute.

Bucket shops abound from coast to coast, but here are a couple of recommendations: **Travel Avenue,** 641 W. Lake Street, Chicago, IL 60606 (tel. 312/876-6866, or toll free 800/333-3335); and **Sunline Express Holidays, Inc.,** 607 Market Street, San Francisco, CA 94105 (tel. 415/541-7800, or toll free 800/SUNLINE).

BY SHIP

CRUISES

Cunard Line, 555 Fifth Avenue, New York, NY 10017 (tel. 212/880-7500, or toll free 800/221-4770), boasts that its flagship, the *Queen Elizabeth 2,* is the only five-star-plus luxury ocean liner providing regular transatlantic service. Many passengers appreciate its graceful introduction to British mores and the absolute lack of jet lag that an ocean crossing can provide.

FREIGHTER

Passage on a freighter tends to be less expensive than on a passenger ship, but you will need to do a little comparison shopping. For example, a budget accommodation aboard the *QE2* can cost less money and get you to England faster than a freighter. For legal reasons, no freighter can carry more than 12 passengers.

For more information on freighter travel, write to **Fords Travel,** 19448 Londelius Street, Northridge, CA 91324 (tel. 818/701-7414).

One company operating freighters is **Mediterranean Shipping Co.,** c/o Sea the Difference, 96 Morton Street, New York, NY 10014 (tel. 212/691-3760, or toll free 800/666-9333), offering year-round voyages from Boston and New York ports to Felixstowe in England.

FERRY & HOVERCRAFT

Many visitors come to London by ferry or Hovercraft from mainland Europe, especially France. The major carriers are **Sealink** (tel. 023/364-7047), **Hoverspeed** (tel. 030/421-6205), and **P&O**

Channel Lines (tel. 081/575-8555). These companies offer ferry service across the Channel from Calais and Boulogne, two ports in France, to the English ports of Dover and Folkestone. Calais to Dover takes 90 minutes, and Boulogne to Folkestone takes 1 hour and 50 minutes. The fastest water crossing from France to England— 40 minutes—is via Hoverspeed's Hovercraft from Boulogne to Dover.

BY TRAIN

If you plan to tour Britain and France, you might consider the **BritFrance Railpass,** which includes round-trip catamaran Channel crossings. You may choose a total of any 5 days of unlimited rail travel during a 15-day consecutive period, or 10 days during a single month—on both the British and French rail networks.

In Paris at the Gare du Nord, you board a French Turbotrain, which will take you to the port of Boulogne. There, at the catamaran terminal, you can board *The Sea Cat,* which will take you to Dover Priory Station on England's south coast. From there you go by Citylink rail into London's Victoria Station. Trip time is 5½ hours.

Americans can secure the pass at **BritRail Travel International-al,** 1500 Broadway, New York, NY 10036 (tel. 212/575-2667). Canadians can write to P.O. Box 89510, 250 Eglinton Avenue East, Toronto, ON M4P 3E1.

ORIENTATION

ARRIVING

BY PLANE   London is served by two major airports: Heathrow and Gatwick; both have good public transport links to central London.

The cheapest route from **Heathrow Airport** is by Underground ("the tube"). The 15-mile journey takes approximately 45 minutes to any downtown station. Service is convenient, since the Underground platforms are directly below the airport's four terminals. Most transatlantic flights arrive (and depart) from Terminals 1 and 2. Terminal 3 services intra-European flights, while Terminal 4 is the long-haul hub for British Airways exclusively. Trains depart every 4 to 10 minutes from 6am to midnight. You can also take Airbus, which departs frequently and takes about an hour to reach central London. The most expensive option would be to take a taxi.

Aside from a taxi, there are two ways of making the 25-mile trip from **Gatwick Airport** to the city center. The first, and more popular, is by express train, which takes 30 minutes to reach Victoria Station. The station is located just below the airport, and trains depart every 15 minutes from 6am to 10pm (hourly, on the hour, at other times). You can also take the Flightline 777 bus operated by Green Line (tel. 081/668-7261). The trip takes 70 minutes. Buses destined for Victoria Coach Station depart from Gatwick's North Terminal hourly, at different times throughout the day.

BY TRAIN Trains from Paris arrive at **Victoria Station** (tel. 071/928-5100, daily 24 hours), visitors from Amsterdam are deposited at **Liverpool Street Station** (tel. 071/928-5100, daily 24 hours), and arrivals from Edinburgh pull into **King's Cross Station** (tel. 071/278-2477, daily 7am–11pm). All three stations are well connected to the city's extensive bus and Underground network. The stations all have London Transport Information Centres, luggage lockers, telephones, restaurants, and pubs.

CITY LAYOUT

NEIGHBORHOODS IN BRIEF

Mayfair Bounded by Piccadilly, Hyde Park, Oxford, and Regent streets, this section of London is considered the most elegant; it encompasses Grosvenor and Berkeley squares.

St. James's Royal London begins at Piccadilly Circus, moving southwest. It basks in its associations with royalty, from the "merrie monarch," Charles II, to today's Queen Elizabeth II.

The Strand and Covent Garden Beginning at Trafalgar Square, the Strand runs east into Fleet Street and is flanked with theaters, shops, hotels, and restaurants. Until 1970 Covent Garden was the fruit, flower, and vegetable market of London. Today it is a major shopping district, with dozens of restaurants and cafés, and site of the Royal Opera House on Bow Street.

Holborn The old borough of Holborn takes in the heart of legal London—home of the city's barristers, solicitors, and law clerks. It contains the ancient Inns of Court.

Westminster/Whitehall This area has been the seat of British government since the days of Edward the Confessor. It is dominated by the Houses of Parliament and Westminster Abbey.

Belgravia South of Hyde Park, this has been the long-time aristocratic quarter of London, rivaling Mayfair in wealth and elegance. It reached its pinnacle of prestige during the reign of Queen

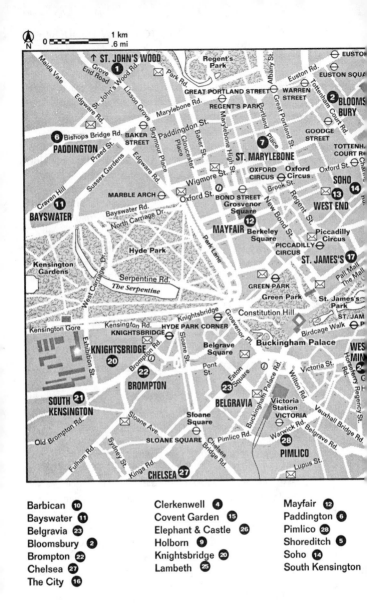

Victoria. It lies near Buckingham Palace Gardens and Brompton Road, and its center is Belgrave Square.

Knightsbridge Adjoining Belgravia, Knightsbridge is a top residential and shopping area, just south of Hyde Park. At its center is the world's most famous department store, Harrods.

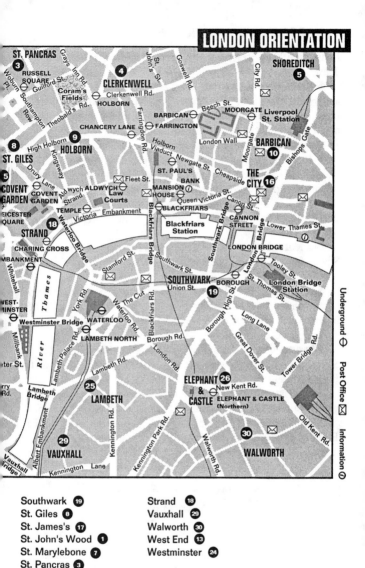

ST. PANCRAS **3**

RUSSELL SQUARE

CLERKENWELL **4**

HOLBORN

SHOREDITCH **5**

Coram's Fields

BARBICAN
FARRINGTON

MOORGATE
Liverpool St. Station

CHANCERY LANE

BARBICAN **10**

8
ST. GILES

HOLBORN **9**

London Wall

THE CITY **16**

ST. PAUL'S

5
COVENT GARDEN

COVENT GARDEN

ALDWYCH
Law Courts

BANK
MANSION HOUSE

EICESTER QUARE

TEMPLE

BLACKFRIARS

STRAND **18**

CHARING CROSS

CANNON STREET

LONDON BRIDGE

MBANKMENT

Blackfriars Station

WEST-MINSTER

Westminster Bridge

WATERLOO

SOUTHWARK
BOROUGH **19**

London Bridge Station

LAMBETH NORTH

ELEPHANT & CASTLE **26**

ELEPHANT & CASTLE (Northern)

25
LAMBETH

30

29
VAUXHALL

WALWORTH

Southwark **19**	Strand **18**
St. Giles **8**	Vauxhall **29**
St. James's **17**	Walworth **30**
St. John's Wood **1**	West End **13**
St. Marylebone **7**	Westminster **24**
St. Pancras **3**	

Underground ⊖   Post Office ⊠   Information ⊖

Chelsea A stylish district stretching along the River Thames, Chelsea lies south of Hyde Park and South Kensington. It begins at Sloane Square, and its best-known and shop-flanked avenue is King's Road.

Kensington A royal borough, Kensington is traversed by

Kensington High Street and encompasses most of Kensington Gardens.

South Kensington   Lying south of Kensington Gardens and Hyde Park, South Kensington, primarily a residential area, is often called "museumland" because of the many museums found here.

Paddington/Bayswater   The Paddington section lies close to Paddington Station, just northwest of Kensington Gardens and Hyde Park. It is a center for budget travelers who are looking for reasonably priced bed-and-breakfasts. Lying just north of Bayswater Road and Kensington Gardens, Bayswater is another center of budget B&Bs, which have often been converted from former private town houses.

St. Marylebone   Below Regent's Park and north of Oxford Street, St. Marylebone is primarily a residential area that faces Mayfair to the south.

Soho   This area of narrow lanes and crooked streets, once the main foreign quarter of London, has some of the city's best international restaurants. Soho starts at Piccadilly Circus and stretches to Oxford Street.

Bloomsbury   To the northeast of Piccadilly Circus, beyond Soho, is Bloomsbury, heart of academic London and site of the British Museum.

The City   In the eastern part of London, this was the original walled Roman City and is today the center of financial London.

The East End   One of London's poorest districts, the East End borders the richer area of the City. Many immigrants have found a home here, but it is most famous for its cockneys.

GETTING AROUND

London's public transportation network is both vast and efficient. In central London, Underground stations abound. Above ground, the city's famous red double-decker buses cross the city in all directions. Both the Underground and buses are operated by London Regional Transport (LRT), which sets fares based on a zone system: You pay for each zone you cross.

London Regional Transport Travel Information Centres are located in most of the major Underground stations, including Heathrow Central, King's Cross, Oxford Circus, Piccadilly Circus, and Victoria. Off-hour times vary, but all provide service weekdays

from 9am to 5pm. LRT also maintains a 24-hour telephone information service (tel. 071/222-1234).

SAVING MONEY   You can save money by purchasing one of
three types of Travelcards. A central London **one-day Travelcard**
is good for unlimited transportation within 3 zones on the bus and
tube after 9:30am Monday through Friday and anytime during
weekends and public holidays. There are also **weekly Travelcards**
and **monthly Travelcards** valid within the Central London Zone.
You will need to present a passport-size photo to buy the weekly or
monthly cards; photo booths are located in Underground stations.

BY UNDERGROUND   Except for Christmas Day, when the
Underground is closed, trains run every few minutes from about
5:30am Monday through Saturday and from 7:30am on Sunday.
Closing times vary with each station, but the last trains always leave
between 11:30pm and midnight. Last train times are posted at the
entrance of each station. Tickets can be purchased at the station
ticket window or from an adjacent coin-operated machine. Hold on
to your ticket throughout your ride; you'll need it to exit. Pick up a
handy tube map, distributed free at station ticket windows.

BY BUS   On the red open-back platform buses, take a seat, either
upstairs or down, and wait for the conductor to collect your fare. On
the newer buses, pay the driver as you enter and exit through the rear
doors.

   Many tourists are reluctant to ride the buses because their routes
can be confusing. Get a free bus map from the tourist office, or just
ask any conductor about the route and take advantage of a "top
deck" sightseeing adventure.

   Regular bus service stops after midnight. Night buses have
different routes and different numbers from their daytime counter-
parts, and service is less frequent; most routes are serviced only once
each hour. Unlike weekly and monthly Travelcards, one-day passes
are not valid on night buses.

BY TAXI   For three or four people traveling a short distance, cabs
can be economical. The city's big black cabs now come in other
colors (primarily maroon), but the ride is still fun. A taxi is available
when the yellow sign on its roof is illuminated. Hail a cab by raising
your arm. The driver will lower the window when he pulls to the curb
so you can state your destination before climbing in. You can hail a
cab on the street or in front of train stations, large hotels, and popular
tourist attractions. If you know in advance you'll be needing a cab,
you can order one by calling 071/253-5000.

FAST FACTS / LONDON

American Express American Express Travel Services has about a dozen offices around the city, including one at 6 Haymarket, SW1 (tel. 071/930-4411) and one at the British Travel Centre, 4 Lower Regent Street, SW1 (tel. 071/839-2682). To report lost or stolen cards at any time, call 071/222-9633.

Area Code The area code is 071 in central London, 081 in outer London. Area codes are necessary when dialing from outside the code. From the United States dial 71 and 81, respectively.

Bookstores Dillon's Bookstore, 82 Gower Street, WC1 (tel. 071/636-1577), is one of the largest and best chain bookshops in town. Hatchards, 187 Piccadilly, W1 (tel. 071/437-3924), known as an upscale bookshop, is another good choice for popular books.

Business Hours Most **banks** are open Monday through Friday. 9:30am to 3:30pm. Some are also open Saturday 9:30am to noon. **Offices** are generally open Monday through Friday from 8:30 or 9am until 5 or 5:30pm. **Stores** are usually open Monday through Saturday 10am to 6pm, but most stay open at least one extra hour one night during the week. By law, most stores are closed Sunday. **Restaurants** usually open for lunch at 11am and stay open until 11pm or midnight. **Pubs** can legally be open Monday through Saturday 11am to 11pm and Sunday noon to 3pm and 7 to 10:30pm. Note, however, that some pubs begin serving later than others, and many observe Sunday hours throughout the week.

Climate The temperature seldom goes above 70° in the summer or below freezing in the winter. Year round there is likely to be a weather forecast of "scattered clouds with sunny periods and showers, possibly heavy at times."

Currency Exchange As a rule, you will get a better rate for traveler's checks than you will for cash. Banks generally offer the best exchange rates, but American Express and Thomas Cook are competitive and do not charge a commission for cashing the traveler's checks of *any* issuer. **American Express** has a number of offices throughout the city (see above). A conveniently located **Thomas Cook** office is at 1 Marble Arch, W1 (tel. 071/837-5275).

Doctors and Dentists If you need a doctor or dentist and your condition is not life-threatening, call the operator (100) and ask for the local police. They will put you in touch with a specialist. You can also visit **Medical Express,** 117A Harley Street W1 (tel. 071/499-1991), a private walk-in clinic that is open Monday through Friday 9am to 6pm and Saturday 9:30am to 2:30pm. **Emergency**

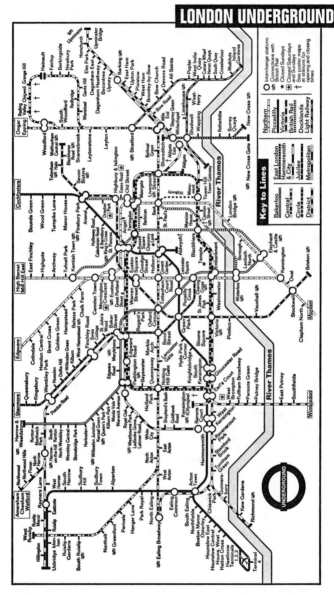

LONDON UNDERGROUND

Dental Service (tel. 071/752-0133), available 24 hours a day, matches dental emergencies with local specialists.

    Drugstores Bliss Chemist, 5 Marble Arch, W1 (tel. 071/723-6116), is open daily 9am to midnight year round. Call the operator (100) and ask the police for the opening hours and addresses of other chemists that stay open late.

Embassies The **U.S. Embassy** is at 24 Grosvenor Square, W1 (tel. 071/499-9000). The **Canadian Embassy** is located at Canada House, Trafalgar Square, WC2 (tel. 071/258-6600). The **Australian High Commission** is at Australia House, The Strand, WC2 (tel. 071/379-4334). The **New Zealand High Commission** can be found at New Zealand House, 80 Haymarket, SW1 (tel. 071/930-8422).

Emergencies Police, fire, or an ambulance can be reached by dialing **999** from any phone. No money is required.

Eyeglasses There are many spectacle shops on Oxford Street, King's Road, and other major shopping streets. Harrods and Selfridges both have opticians on duty and offer a good selection of frames. The **Contact Lens Centre,** 32 Camden High Street, NW1 (tel. 071/383-3838), is one of the least expensive shops for both contact lenses and regular eyeglasses.

Holidays Most businesses are closed December 25 and 26, January 1, Good Friday, Easter Monday, and May 1. In addition, many stores close on bank holidays, which are scattered throughout the year.

Hospitals In an emergency, dial **999** from any phone; no money is needed. **University College Hospital,** Gower Street, W1 (tel. 071/387-9300), is one of the most centrally located. A dozen other city hospitals also offer 24-hour walk-in emergency care. Dial 100 and ask the operator to connect you with the police; they will tell you which one is closest.

Hotlines **Capital Helpline** (tel. 071/388-7575) enables you to speak with someone who will answer any legitimate question about London. The **Samaritans,** 46 Marshall Street, W1 (tel. 071/734-2800), maintains a 24-hour crisis hotline to help with almost any kind of trouble. **Alcoholics Anonymous** (tel. 071/352-3001) offers a daily hotline from 10am–10pm.

Libraries The British Library, Great Russell Street, WC1 (tel. 071/636-1544), is one of the largest in the world, holding at least one copy of every book published in Britain. Since this library may not serve the needs of the casual reader, the helpful staff can direct you to one of the city's more accessible or specialized libraries. **Westminster Central Reference Library,** St. Martin's Street, WC2 (tel. 071/798-2034), has the city's best collection of reference materials and periodicals. It is open to the public weekdays and Saturday.

Lost Property If you lose something on the bus or Underground, wait two days and then contact the **London Transport Lost Property Office,** 200 Baker St., NW1 (tel. 071/486-2496).

Belongings left in taxis may have been turned over to the **Metropolitan Police Lost Property Office,** 15 Penton Street, N1 (tel. 071/833-0996). There are also lost-property offices at all major British Rail stations.

Newspapers/Magazines The *Times,* the *Telegraph,* the *Daily Mail,* and the *Guardian* are all London papers that carry the latest news. The *International Herald Tribune,* published in Paris, and an international edition of *USA Today,* beamed via satellite, are available daily. Copies of *Time* and *Newsweek* are also sold at most newsstands. Small magazines, such as *Time Out* and *City Limits,* contain much useful data about the latest happenings in London, including theatrical and cultural events.

Photographic Needs The **Flash Centre,** 54 Brunswick Centre, WC1 (tel. 071/837-6163), is considered the best professional photographic equipment supplier in London. **Dixons,** 88 Oxford Street, W1 (tel. 071/636-8511), with more than 80 branches throughout the city, carries a large inventory of photographic supplies.

Police In an emergency, dial **999** from any phone; no money is needed. At other times, dial the operator (100) and ask to be connected with the police.

Post Office Post offices and subpost offices are centrally located and open Monday through Friday 9am to 5:30pm, Saturday 9:30am to noon. The **Chief Post Office** in London is at King Edward Street, EC1 (tel. 071/239-5047).

Restrooms Well-maintained public restrooms can be found in such places as museums, art galleries, large department stores, and railway stations. Beige-and-silver automatic toilets, found on many streets, are inexpensive and are sterilized after each use.

Safety It is best to use discretion and keep to well-lit areas. Always be aware of your immediate surroundings. Wear a moneybelt and pay close attention to your possessions, whether you are walking on the street or sitting in a pub or restaurant. Be particularly careful with cameras, purses, and wallets, all favorite targets for thieves and pickpockets.

Shoe Repair Most of the major Underground stations have "heel bars" that can make quick repairs. More extensive work can be performed in any of the major department stores or at **Jeeves Snob Shop,** 8–10 Pont Street, SW1 (tel. 071/235-1101).

Taxes In England, a Value-Added Tax (VAT) is included in the price of nearly everything you might buy—hotel accommodations, meals, gifts, souvenirs. Tourists may be able to get a VAT refund for major purchases.

Telephone and Fax London now has two area codes (see

above). Generally, you will find two kinds of pay phones—one accepts coins and the other requires a Phonecard (which can be purchased from a newsagent). Phonecard telephones automatically deduct the cost of your call from the card. Some large hotels also have credit-card telephones that accept major credit cards. Lift the handle and follow the instructions on the screen.

To reach the **local operator,** dial 100. The **international operator** is 155. **London phone information** (Directory Inquiries) can be reached by dialing 142 and is free of charge.

If you need to send a fax and your hotel has no facilities, contact **Chesham Executive Centre,** 150 Regent Street, W1 (tel. 071/439-6288).

Tipping Most **restaurants** routinely add a service charge (the restaurant's policy will be written on the menu). If the service charge is *not* included, a 10% to 15% tip is customary. **Taxi drivers** expect 10% to 15% of the fare. Note that tipping is rare in both pubs and theaters.

Tourist Information The **London Tourist Board** operates Tourist Information Centres at several locations, including the Victoria Station Forecourt, SW1. This one is open Monday through Saturday 8:00am to 7:00pm, Sunday 8:00am to 4:00pm. Telephone inquiries may be made by calling **London Information** at 071/730-3488.

Transit Information The **London Regional Transport (LRT) Travel Information Service** (tel. 071/222-1234) offers schedule and fare information for bus, Underground, and British Rail service within Greater London. Open 24 hours.

The City

Start: Bank Underground Station.
Finish: St. Paul's Cathedral.
Time: 2½ hours.
Best Times: Weekdays from 10am to 4pm.
Worst Times: Nights and weekends (when many buildings are closed).

The City of London, which occupies an area of approximately one square mile, was established by the Romans, who then built a protective wall around it in the 2nd century A.D. Entrance to the City was via a series of gates now commemorated in street names such as New Gate, Alders (older) Gate, and the like. Other street names in the City derive from the goods and services that were traded there, including Bread Street, Wood Street, and even Love Lane. Some are named for their most impressive features, such as Turnagain Lane and Stinking Lane.

In the early Middle Ages, the City asserted its independence from royal jurisdiction; it established an autonomous government with a Lord Mayor and a court of aldermen (elders). Today, the City remains

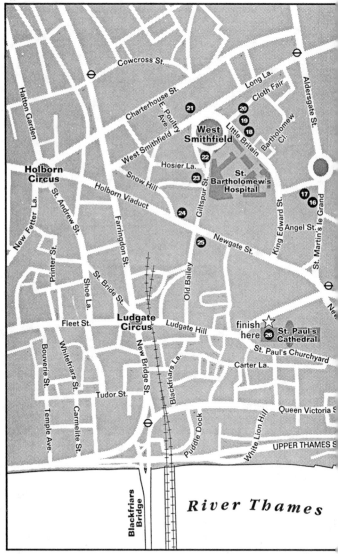

Map labels

- Cowcross St.
- Charterhouse St.
- Long La.
- Cloth Fair
- Aldersgate St.
- Hatton Garden
- E. Poultry Ave.
- West Smithfield
- **West Smithfield**
- Little Britain
- St. Bartholomew Cl.
- **Holborn Circus**
- Hosier La.
- St. Bartholomew's Hospital
- Snow Hill
- Holborn Viaduct
- Giltspur St.
- King Edward St.
- Angel St.
- St. Martin's le Grand
- New Fetter La.
- St. Andrew St.
- Printer St.
- Newgate St.
- Shoe La.
- St. Bride St.
- Farringdon St.
- Old Bailey
- Fleet St.
- **Ludgate Circus**
- Ludgate Hill
- finish here
- **St. Paul's Cathedral**
- St. Paul's Churchyard
- Bouverie St.
- Whitefriars St.
- New Bridge St.
- Blackfriars La.
- Carter La.
- Queen Victoria S
- Tudor St.
- Temple Ave.
- Carmelite St.
- Puddle Dock
- White Lion Hill
- UPPER THAMES S
- Blackfriars Bridge
- *River Thames*

0 ——— 220 y
      201 m
N

① The Royal Exchange
② The Bank of England
③ The Stock Exchange
④ Mansion House
⑤ The Temple of Mithras
⑥ Ye Old Watling
⑦ Bow Lane
⑧ St. Mary-le-Bow Church
⑨ The Statue of Captain John Smith
⑩ Cheapside
⑪ Wood Street
⑫ The Wood Street Comptor
⑬ Guildhall
⑭ Love Lane
⑮ The Roman Fort and City Wall

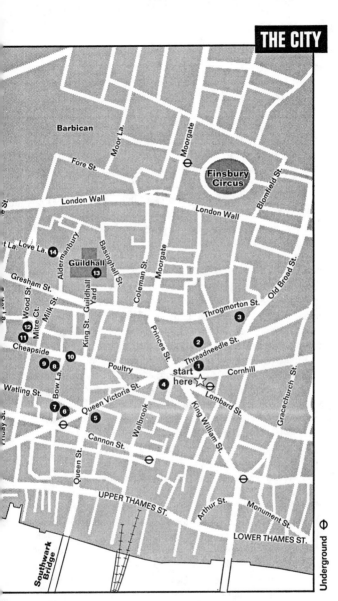

THE CITY

Barbican

Moor La.

Moorgate

Fore St.

Finsbury
Circus

Blomfield St.

London Wall

London Wall

t La. Love La.

14

Aldermanbury

Basinghall St.

Coleman St.

Moorgate

Old Broad St.

Guildhall

13

Gresham St.

Wood St.

Mitre Ct.

Milk St.

King St.

Guildhall
Yard

Throgmorton St.

3

12

11

Cheapside

10

2

Threadneedle St.

1

9 8

Bow La.

Poultry

start
here

Cornhill

Watling St.

7 6

Queen Victoria St.

5

4

Walbrook

Lombard St.

Gracechurch St.

Friday St.

Cannon St.

Queen St.

King William St.

UPPER THAMES ST.

Arthur St.

Monument St.

LOWER THAMES ST.

Underground

Southwark
Bridge

both the financial center of England, and an autonomous precinct not subject to the laws of the monarch. Many of the winding, narrow streets have changed little over the centuries, making this part of London one of the most interesting for walking.

Leave Bank Underground Station and cross Cornhill. You will be at an intersection in the City where you can see three of Britain's most important financial institutions. To your right is:

1. The Royal Exchange, which was founded by Sir Thomas Gresham in the mid-16th century for the purpose of trading wholesale and retail goods. The present building, designed by Sir William Tite, dates from 1844. Since 1972, when world currencies were floated, this building has been the headquarters for the London International Financial Futures Exchange (LIFFE).

Cross Threadneedle Street to:

2. The Bank of England. The building, designed by Sir John Soane, was erected between 1788 and 1833. A new complex was added by Sir Herbert Baker in the period between the two world wars. Known as the "Old Lady of Threadneedle Street," the bank is both a central bank—managing the public debt and serving as a depository for government funds—and the institution that issues bank notes for general circulation.

The bank was established "for the Publick Good and Benefit of Our People" in 1694, when a Royal Charter was granted by King William III and Queen Mary II. Although it carried out governmental functions, the bank remained privately owned until 1946. **The Bank of England Museum** (tel. 071/601-4878) is open to the public Monday through Friday from 10am to 5pm; admission is free).

With the bank on your left, cross Bartholomew Lane and bear left to:

3. The Stock Exchange, Old Broad Street. Founded in 1773, the Stock Exchange is now located in a modern glass building that was erected in the early 1970s. Although there is a visitors center, where you can listen to a short lecture on how the market functions, the actual transactions have, since 1986, been carried out electronically. The visitors center is open Monday through Friday from 9:30am to 3:30pm; admission is free.

Retrace your steps to the intersection of Cornhill and Threadneedle Street. Cross Cornhill and King William Street. To your left is:

4. Mansion House, the official residence of the Lord Mayor, which was built by George Dance the Elder between 1739 and 1753. The Corinthian columns form an impressive backdrop for the Lord Mayor's appearance at ceremonial functions. The main reception room—Egyptian Hall—is the setting for official banquets.

With Mansion House to your left, walk 2 blocks down Queen Victoria Street to the ruins of:

5. The Temple of Mithras. Mithraism, an ancient Persian cult that was introduced to London by Roman soldiers, became widely accepted during the 2nd century A.D. The temple was erected in the 3rd century, when the religion was at the height of its popularity. Probably the building was destroyed in the 4th century, when the Roman Empire under Constantine accepted Christianity (many pagan temples were torn down at that time). The temple's former entrance is to your right at the end of the central nave (which is lined with columns dividing it into aisles). The temple was discovered in 1954 when developers were excavating a new building site. Sculptures and other objects from the temple are now on display at the Museum of London.

Walk back 1 block to the traffic light and cross the street to Watling Street, located on the opposite side of this busy intersection. Half a block ahead you'll see:

6. Ye Olde Watling, 29 Watling Street (tel. 071/248-6252). Built in 1668 by Sir Christopher Wren, London's most famous architect, this atmospheric old pub was constructed with wood taken from dismantled sailing ships. The pub served as Wren's office during the construction of nearby St. Paul's Cathedral. Good lunches are available, as well as Bass, IPA, Best Bitter, and other beers.

Cross Watling Street onto:

7. Bow Lane, a charming little pedestrian thoroughfare that evokes the medieval period. Before the 16th century, this lane was called "Cordwainers Street," for the shoemakers and leather workers who lived and traded here, but then it was renamed for the nearby church.

Half a block down Bow Lane, turn left into Groveland Court to find:

REFUELING STOP   Williamson's Tavern, Groveland Court (tel. 071/248-6280). In the 17th century, this building was the official residence of the Lord Mayor of the City of London. The wrought iron gates in front were presented to the Lord Mayor by King William III and Queen Mary II. Inside, you'll see a fireplace constructed of ancient Roman tiles that were discovered on this site when the pub was erected. A stone marker on the tavern floor supposedly designates the exact center of the City. The pub is famous with the locals for its terrific steak sandwiches.

Walk half a block and turn left into Bow Churchyard, adjacent to:

8. St. Mary-le-Bow Church, Cheapside. Traditionally, an authentic cockney was defined as someone who was born within hearing range of the Bow bells. The first mention of this church traces back to 1091, when it was recorded that the roof blew off in a storm—the beginning of what seemed to be a string of bad luck. In 1196 William Fitz Osbert was smoked out of the church's tower after murdering one of the Archbishop of Canterbury's guards. In 1271, the tower fell, killing 20 people. In 1284, a local goldsmith was murdered in this church. In 1331, a balcony, on which Queen Phillipa (wife of King Edward III) stood, collapsed, injuring her highness and several of her attendants. Finally, the church was burned in the Great Fire of 1666. Rebuilt by Sir Christopher Wren, the present building was modeled after the Church of the Basilica of Maxentius in Rome. The 217-foot steeple is widely considered to be Wren's finest. Step inside and look at the capitals on top the support columns. Each one has a stone relief of the World War II allied heads of state, including Winston Churchill, Charles de Gaulle, and Franklin D. Roosevelt. Downstairs, you can visit the old Norman crypt whose bowed Norman arches gave this church its name.

Exit the church and take a look at:

9. The Statue of Captain John Smith, located on the square just outside the main entrance. Smith, a parishioner of St. Mary-le-Bow, was among the first colonists to settle Jamestown, Virginia.

The street in front of the church is:

10. Cheapside, formerly one of the busiest commercial streets in London. From the 13th to 17th centuries this thoroughfare was a bustling marketplace for jewelry, shoes, bread, meat, spices, wine, and all kinds of trinkets and supplies. Its name derives from the Anglo-Saxon word *ceap* (or *chepe*), meaning "to barter." This is the origin of the modern word "cheap," and "shopping" evolved from the word "cheping."

Cheapside's timber-framed shops were destroyed by the Great Fire of 1666, after which the street was widened and lined with loftier buildings. The expansion of London in the late 18th and 19th centuries gave rise to a rival shopping area—Oxford

Street, which is now one of the city's most important shopping streets.

Turn left onto Cheapside and take the first right onto:

11. Wood Street, London's former timber-selling center. Look up at the large **plane tree** that can be seen behind the buildings at the corner of Cheapside. This tree was immortalized by the Romantic poet William Wordsworth in "The Reverie of Poor Susan":

> *At the corner of Wood Street*
> *   when daylight appears*
> *Hangs a thrush that sings loud,*
> *It has sung for three years.*
> *Poor Susan has passed by the*
> *   spot, and has heard*
> *In the silence of morning,*
> *   the song of the bird.*

Walk 1 block down Wood Street and turn right into Mitre Court. The glass canopy on your right covers:

12. The Wood Street Comptor, a debtor's prison during the 16th and 17th centuries. Unlike modern-day jails, comptors were semiprivate enterprises; prisoners had to pay for their accommodations, meals, wine, and various services. This comptor was divided into three sections: the Master's Side, for wealthy inmates; the Knight's Side, for those of moderate means; and The Hole, for debtors who were really poor. The Wood Street Comptor is rarely open to the public, but if you ask politely at the Vinters Off-License next door, they might let you go down the steps to see the dungeons.

Exit Mitre Court via the passageway opposite the one you entered. Turn left down Milk Street, then right onto Gresham Street and almost directly ahead—to the side of the church—a small passageway leads you to:

13. Guildhall, the City of London's City Hall, and the seat of·the Lord Mayor and the Court of Aldermen since the 12th century (tel. 071/606-3030). The present building was completed in 1439, but it was severely damaged in the Great Fire of 1666. and again by German bombers in December 1940. In the Great Hall one can see the banners with the coats-of-arms of various City craft guilds such as the Barbers, Brewers, Fishmongers, Glovers, and Gunmakers. Beneath the hall is the largest medieval crypt in London. The Guildhall also contains an extensive library with thousands of items of historical and literary interest. The **Clock**

Museum displays exhibits on the history of clockmaking. The Guildhall is open to the public Monday through Friday from 10am to 4pm and on occasional weekends.

Return to Gresham Street, turn right, and take your first right into Aldermanbury. After 1 block, turn left into:

14. Love Lane, and enter the gardens on your right. Once populated by prostitutes, this street was named for the services that were sold here. The church of St. Mary Aldermanbury was formerly located on the site of these gardens until it was dismantled and moved to Westminster College in Fulton, Missouri, in the 1960s. The bust hidden in the bushes is that of Shakespeare, with an inscribed tribute to John Heminges and Henry Condell, editors of the Bard's first folio of his complete works (1623).

Walk 1 block to the end of the lane, cross the road and continue ahead into the narrow passageway. Exit the passageway and turn right into Oat Lane. Walk 1 block ahead and cross Noble Street; you will then see the remains of:

15. The Roman Fort and City Wall, which are among the oldest structures in London. Built around A.D. 120, the fort originally covered 12 acres and was built to accommodate the guards of the Roman Governor of Britain. At least 1,000 men were housed in the fort's barracks. These remaining walls were part of the curved southwest corner watch tower.

With the fort on your right, walk 1 block up Noble Street and turn right onto Gresham Street. Turn right onto St. Martin's le Grand and 2 blocks ahead, on your left, you will see:

16. St. Botolph Church, one of three City churches dedicated to the patron saint of travelers. Each St. Botolph church is located near the former site of a City gate—in this case, Aldersgate. If the church is open, you can explore its interesting interior, complete with a splendid barrel-vaulted roof and sword rests for the parishioners.

Walk through the gate to the left of the church and you're in:

17. Postman's Park, named for its proximity to the General Post Office. Walk straight ahead to the small monument with the red terra-cotta roof. This is a national memorial commemorating acts of heroism by ordinary men and women. Dedicated in 1910, the monument is covered with epitaphs to unsung heroes such as John Cranmer, aged 23, who "drowned off Ostend whilst saving the life of a stranger and a foreigner."

Continue straight through the park and exit via the gate opposite the one you entered. Turn right onto Little Britain and walk 3 blocks to:

18. **The Gatehouse of St. Bartholomew the Great,** Smithfield Square. Take a step back to admire this stunning old church entrance. Above the gate is one of the earliest surviving timber-frame house fronts in London. It was built by William Scudamore in 1595 and restored in 1916 after damage from a Zeppelin bomb. Parts of the stone gate date from 1240, but most of the stonework was installed during restoration in 1932.

Walk through the gatehouse and straight into:

19. **The Church of St. Bartholomew the Great.** This is London's oldest parish church, part of an Augustinian priory founded in 1123 by a monk named Thomas Rahere (who, according to tradition, was also the court jester). The church was spared from the Great Fire of 1666 as well as the bombing during World War II. Just inside the door, on your right, are the church's cloisters, which date from the 15th century. Walk straight into the main part of the church and look carefully at the carvings on the right wall. One of these statues created a lot of excitement in the 18th century when "tears" were found rolling down the figure's face; it hasn't happened again, perhaps due to the installation of a dry-heating unit in the church.

In 1539 King Henry VIII confiscated all of this church's property, which was then used for stables, a private home, and a printing office where Benjamin Franklin worked in 1725.

Exit the church from the same door you entered; turn right and go up the steps. The street just ahead is:

20. **Cloth Fair,** site of the Bartholomew Fair, a sort of medieval street carnival that was held annually from 1123 to 1855. The house with colored panels beneath its windows—Number 41—dates from 1647, making it one of the few remaining London buildings that survived the Great Fire of 1666.

REFUELING STOP   The Rising Sun, 38 Cloth Fair (tel. 071/726-6671). Located directly opposite the Church of St. Bartholomew the Great graveyard, this 18th-century pub was once frequented by an infamous gang of body snatchers; they drugged drunk strangers and sold their bodies to doctors at nearby St. Bartholomew's Hospital. The food here isn't particularly noteworthy, but the beer and the company are good, making this pub one of our favorite area hangouts.

Leave the pub and turn right, down the alleyway called Rising Sun Court. The large building across the street is:

21. **Smithfield Market,** a 10-acre, cast-iron Victorian structure

housing Europe's largest meat market. Trading in sheep, pigs, cattle, and poultry started here in 1173. In the 19th century, the livestock market was moved to Islington, leaving these sawdust-covered floors exclusively to the butcher trade. Trading occurs throughout the night and finishes around daybreak.

Facing the market, turn left onto Long Lane; after 1 block, turn left again onto West Smithfield and walk around the square to Giltspur Street. The stone gate on your left is the:

22. **Henry VIII Gateway,** the entrance to St. Bartholomew's, England's oldest hospital. Constructed in 1702, the gate was a gift to the hospital from the stonemasons who worked on St. Paul's Cathedral. London's only statue of Henry VIII stands atop the gate—a tribute to the king who opened the hospital to the public. Incidentally, it was in the pathology department of St. Bart's hospital where Sir Arthur Conan Doyle's Dr. Watson met Sherlock Holmes.

Continue 1 block up Giltspur Street and look up at the small statue on the building at the right-hand corner of Cock Lane. This is:

23. **The Fat Boy** (or Golden Boy), erected by the City of London together with a plaque that reads: "This boy is in memory put up to the late Fire of London, occasioned by the sin of gluttony 1666." Popular myth holds that the Great Fire was God's way of punishing overindulgent Londoners.

Continue 1 block to the end of Giltspur Street, turn right onto Holborn Viaduct, and enter:

24. **The Church of the Holy Sepulchre.** Founded in 1137 just outside the City wall's Northern Gate, the church was the departure point for the knights of the Crusades. It was named after the Holy Sepulchre Church in Jerusalem, the Crusaders' destination.

The present building dates from 1450; it was erected during the reign of Henry VI. Famous people who are buried here include John Rogers, the first English Protestant to be burned for his faith; and Captain John Smith, the first Governor of Virginia (a brass plate on the south wall describes his escapades).

Inside the church you will also see a 17th-century handbell that used to be rung each night before an execution at nearby Newgate Prison. Shakespeare refers to this ritual in *Macbeth* as "the fatal belman that gives the sternest goodnight of all."

Leave the church and turn left onto Holborn Viaduct (which becomes Newgate Street). Across the street, at the corner of Giltspur Street, is:

REFUELING STOP   The Viaduct Tavern, 126 Newgate Street. When it was built in 1868, this pretty copper-ceiling pub advertised "drunk for a penny, but dead drunk for tuppence." Notice the small hole in the canvas wall painting: It was made by a bullet that missed its intended target—one of two World War I soldiers who got into an argument. By way of food, the tavern offers sausages, sandwiches, and hot meat pies. In addition to Tetley and Burton, there are usually special rotating "guest" beers.

Directly across from the pub is:

25. The Old Bailey Courthouse. Known officially as the "Central Criminal Court," the world-famous Old Bailey is actually the name of the street on which the court stands. The rather nondescript building occupies the site of the former Newgate Prison which was demolished in 1902. Inside you can witness trials, complete with judges in wigs and flowing robes. The courtrooms are open to the public Monday through Friday from 10am to 1pm and again from 2pm to 4pm. Be warned that cameras are not allowed in the building.

Leave the Old Bailey from the same doors you entered, turn left onto Newgate Street and left again onto Old Bailey. After 5 blocks, turn left onto Ludgate Hill, cross Ave Maria Lane (named for the many religious processions held here in the Middle Ages), and continue half a block to:

26. St. Paul's Cathedral, St. Paul's Churchyard (tel. 071/248-2705). Dedicated to the patron saint of the City of London, St. Paul's is the masterpiece of its architect, Sir Christopher Wren. Wren is buried in the cathedral's crypt; his tomb bears the Latin inscription: "Lector, si monumentum requiris, circumspice" ("Reader, if you seek his monument, look around you"). More than 515 feet long and 365 feet high (from curb to cross), the great Renaissance edifice is capped by one of the largest domes in Christendom. If you still have enough energy, climb the 259 steps to the Whispering Gallery, located just below the dome. The acoustics here are such that even soft sounds can be heard on the other side of the dome, 107 feet away. Within the cathedral, the American Memorial Chapel pays tribute to the thousands of American soldiers who lost their lives in Britain during World War II. Although St. Paul's suffered severe damage during the Blitz, it escaped the total destruction of the surrounding neighborhood. The cathedral has been the setting for many important ceremonies, including the funerals of Admiral Lord Nelson (1806) and Sir Winston Churchill (1965), and the wedding of Prince Charles and Lady Diana Spencer (1981). The cathedral is open Monday through Friday from 10am to 4:15pm, Saturday from 11am to 4:15pm, and Sunday for services only.

WALKING TOUR 2

Dickens's London

Start: Holborn Underground Station.
Finish: Dickens's House.
Time: 2½ hours.
Best Times: Monday through Friday from 1 to 4:30pm, when all the interiors on this tour are open.
Worst Times: Weekends (when much of the route is closed to the general public).

Charles John Huffam Dickens was born in Portsmouth, England, in February 1812. He came to London as a young boy and went to work at Warren's Blacking Warehouse, a boot-polish maker. Dickens lived most of his life in London, and despite, or because of, his profound love/hate relationship for this city, his best works were written here. Dickens loved to walk around London for hours on end, and his novels often read like Victorian-era walking tours. The author's settings in certain neighborhoods are intimately linked to such works as *Little Dorrit*, *The Pickwick Papers*, and *David*

Copperfield. It is claimed that Dickens had a photographic memory, and it may be true. Perhaps more than any other English novelist, Dickens relished elaborate detail and he packed his novels with the sights and sounds of the everyday London he knew. Over and beyond the stories themselves, Dickens provided an accurate insight into London life in the mid-19th century.

Although you will not see the deplorable conditions that prevailed in Dickens's time (for example, overcrowded alleyways, grimy buildings, and coal pollution), you will discover unexpected places of beauty—hidden passageways and courtyards that Dickens knew and loved.

Exit Holborn Underground Station, turn left onto Kingsway, and left again to Remnant Street. One block ahead is:

1. **Lincoln's Inn Fields,** London's largest square. Once farmlands belonging to the Duchess of Portsmouth, Dickens knew these fields well and featured them in his novel *Barnaby Rudge*.

Turn right onto Lincoln's Inn Fields and walk half a block to:

2. **John Forster's House,** 58 Lincoln's Inn Fields. Originally constructed in 1730, the house was divided into two in the 1790s, at which time the ornate porch was added. John Forster, a lawyer, as well as the Book and Drama Editor of *The Examiner,* lived here from 1834 to 1856. One of Dickens's best friends, as well as trusted confidant, Forster often accompanied Dickens on rambunctious rambles around the city. They often discussed work, and Dickens relied on Forster for business and creative advice. Forster went on to become Dickens's primary biographer.

In the book *Bleak House*, Dickens modeled the home of Mr. Tulkinghorn, a sinister lawyer, on this very house. Dickens describes it as "a large house, formerly a house of state . . . let off in chambers now; and in those shrunken fragments of greatness lawyers lie like maggots in nuts. . . ."

On December 2, 1844, in an upstairs room, Dickens gave a private reading from his sentimental Christmas novel *The Chimes*. The select gathering of literary figures included Wilkie Collins, the novelist and author of *The Woman in White*. The reading proved such a success that Dickens decided to repeat it three days later. From these informal gatherings, Dickens went on to public readings, which were so popular that he continued them all over Britain and later took them to America. These exhausting trips may have contributed to his premature death in 1870 at just 58 years of age.

Walk counterclockwise around Lincoln's Inn Fields, cross

Sir John Soane's Museum
13 Lincoln Inn Fields
Tues-Sat 10-5

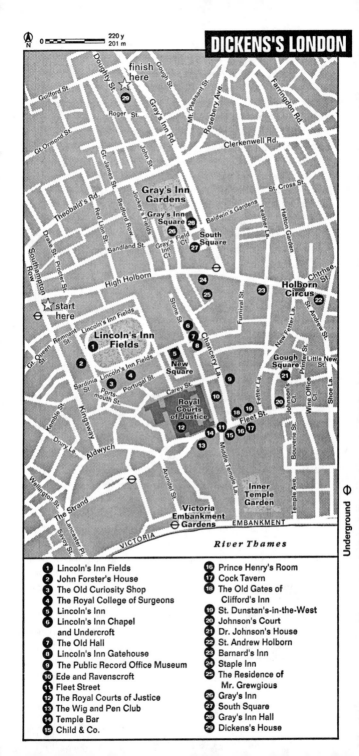

DICKENS'S LONDON

220 y
201 m

Underground ⊖

1. Lincoln's Inn Fields
2. John Forster's House
3. The Old Curiosity Shop
4. The Royal College of Surgeons
5. Lincoln's Inn
6. Lincoln's Inn Chapel and Undercroft
7. The Old Hall
8. Lincoln's Inn Gatehouse
9. The Public Record Office Museum
10. Ede and Ravenscroft
11. Fleet Street
12. The Royal Courts of Justice
13. The Wig and Pen Club
14. Temple Bar
15. Child & Co.
16. Prince Henry's Room
17. Cock Tavern
18. The Old Gates of Clifford's Inn
19. St. Dunstan's-in-the-West
20. Johnson's Court
21. Dr. Johnson's House
22. St. Andrew Holborn
23. Barnard's Inn
24. Staple Inn
25. The Residence of Mr. Grewgious
26. Gray's Inn
27. South Square
28. Gray's Inn Hall
29. Dickens's House

Sardinia Street, and continue straight to Portsmouth Street. A few yards down on the left you will find:

3. The Old Curiosity Shop, 13–14 Portsmouth Street (tel. 071/405-9891). Predecessors of today's variety stores, curiosity shops sold such items as quill pens, paper, and other necessities and novelties. Constructed in 1567 from the wood of dismantled ships, this building was originally used as two farm laborers' cottages, and the land was owned by the Duchess of Portsmouth. Remodeled as one building in the 18th century, this store now has the distinction of being the oldest shop in London.

In Dickens's day, this store was owned by a bookbinder named Tessyman. It is believed that Tessyman's granddaughter inspired Dickens to create the child heroine "Little Nell" for his novel *The Old Curiosity Shop*. Although Dickens wrote that the actual shop he "immortalized" was demolished in his lifetime, he would certainly have been familiar with this old building. The shop experienced financial difficulties in the early 1990s, and its fate is somewhat uncertain. If it is still open, be sure to climb the rickety stairs to the second floor where you'll see the shop's original fireplace.

Return to Lincoln's Inn Fields and turn right, walking counterclockwise around the square. The wonderfully ornate building on your right is:

4. The Royal College of Surgeons, 35 Lincoln's Inn Fields. This impressive building, which dates from the 1830s, was designed by the architect Charles Barry, who also designed the Houses of Parliament. Dickens refers to this building in *Bleak House,* when Mr. Boythorn comments that all lawyers should have their "necks rung and their skulls arranged in Surgeons Hall, for the contemplation of the whole profession, in order that its younger members might understand from actual measurement in early life, how thick skulls may become!"

Exit Lincoln's Inn Fields through the gates just ahead and enter:

5. Lincoln's Inn. This compound is home to one of London's four Inns of Court, societies to which all aspiring and practicing barristers belong. These institutions, dating back to the 14th century, were called "inns" because they provided room and board for their students. Today, tradition still requires legal apprentices to dine with their fraternity 24 times before they are admitted to the bar. Practicing barristers must also continue to dine with the society at least three times during each law term in order to maintain their membership. Unlike solicitors, who prepare the briefs for the cases, barristers (wearing wigs and robes) have a monopoly on pleading in the higher English courts.

As you pass through the gates, look at the building immediately to your left. This is Lincoln's Inn New Hall, the barristers' dining hall, built in 1843. On the right is New Square, an office complex of barristers' chambers, which dates from the 1620s.

Once past the dining hall, turn down the driveway on your left. The small, attractive Gothic building directly ahead of you is the gardener's shed, known locally as "The Head Gardener's Castle." Take the first right down a small pathway, walk up three steps, and you will be standing under:

6. Lincoln's Inn Chapel and Undercroft. It is believed that the chapel was designed by Inigo Jones, one of London's most famous architects. In 1619, the building's foundation stone was laid by the renowned metaphysical poet and preacher John Donne, who also presided over the chapel's consecration on Ascension Day 1623. The covered walkway was intended to be a place where students could "walk and talk and confer for their learning," as well as a private spot where barristers could meet their clients. Several tombstones are scattered around the undercroft—a covered, cloister-like walkway—including that of John Thurloe, Secretary of State under Oliver Cromwell (Lord Protector, 1653–1658).

At the top of the steps, turn right, go down the steps, then bear right out of the cloisters and turn left into the courtyard. The building on your right is:

7. The Old Hall, Lincoln's Inn, an aptly named building dating from the second half of the 15th century. From 1737 to 1875, the Hall housed the High Court of Chancery, England's court of finance and property. Dickens disliked the Court of Chancery, since he had worked there as a court reporter. The Old Hall and the Court of Chancery were targeted by Dickens's vitriolic pen in several novels; perhaps the most scathing description appeared in *Bleak House,* which told of the trial of *Jarndyce* v. *Jarndyce,* a case that had begun so long ago that no one could remember what it was about.

"This is the Court of Chancery; which has its decaying houses and its blighted lands in every shire; which has its worn-out lunatic in every madhouse, and its dead in every churchyard; which has its ruined suitor, with his slipshod heels and threadbare dress, borrowing and begging through the round of every man's acquaintance; which gives to monied might the means abundantly of wearying out the right; which so exhausts finances, patience, courage, hope; so overthrows the brain and breaks the heart; that there is not an honourable man among its practitioners who would not give—who does not often give—the warning, 'Suffer any wrong that can be done you, rather than come here!' "

Visitors are usually not allowed into The Old Hall, but if the doors are open (which often happens), it can't hurt to try to look in.

Walk straight across the courtyard to:

8. Lincoln's Inn Gatehouse, a security gate built between 1517 and 1521 by Sir Thomas Lovell, the son of Henry VIII's chancellor. Lovell's coat of arms can be seen above the doors, together with those of Henry VIII and the Earl of Lincoln, this area's former landowner. According to the biographer John Forster, when Dickens was a young boy, he was walking through this gate when "a big blackguard fellow walked up to me, doffed my cap and said 'hulloa soldier,' which I could not stand so I at once struck him and he then hit me in the eye."

Your journey should be less troublesome as you walk through the gate and turn right onto Chancery Lane. Continue straight for 2 blocks until you reach:

9. The Public Record Office Museum, Chancery Lane (tel. 081/876-2230). Once the main repository for state records, birth certificates, wills, land contracts, and other documents, this historical museum is now devoted exclusively to archives—most records date back before 1782. Documents relating to major events in the history of England are on permanent display, including Shakespeare's will and the Domesday Book.

One block ahead, on your right, is:

10. Ede and Ravenscroft, 93 Chancery Lane, one of the largest outfitters supplying stockings, robes, wigs, and patent leather buckled shoes to local lawyers.

At the end of Chancery Lane, turn right onto:

11. Fleet Street, which immediately becomes The Strand. Named for a river—now covered over—that used to flow along here from Hampstead, Fleet Street is synonymous with journalism, and once accommodated the printing facilities and offices of most London newspapers. Dickens knew this area as such, and surely walked along this street regularly. Since the *Daily Telegraph* and the *Daily Express* moved from their respective buildings several years ago, no newspapers are headquartered here now.

Walk 1 block to:

12. The Royal Courts of Justice. Designed and built by

architect George Street between 1872 and 1882, the courts have a distinctly religious feel about them. Frustrated that he was never commissioned to build a cathedral, Street (according to legend) was able to fulfill his dream vicariously through this building. The spectacular Gothic building was erected with about 35 million bricks, and has more than 1,000 rooms and about 3½ miles of corridors. Stand directly outside the main entrance; look up and you'll see a sculpture of Christ, flanked by statues of King Solomon (left) and King Alfred (right).

Inside the main hall of this high English court is a small exhibit of the official garments worn by judges and barristers. You are free to walk around the building and glance into the courtrooms. Here, and in the halls, you can see the judges dressed in ermine-trimmed robes and full-bottomed wigs. Cameras are not allowed inside.

REFUELING STOP   You can rub elbows with judges and lawyers at **The George,** 213 The Strand (tel. 071/353-9238), an old timbered inn opposite the Royal Courts of Justice. This bilevel pub serves traditional ales on the ground floor and full lunches upstairs. It is known for its good carved meats, served with potatoes and two vegetables.

With your back to the courts, cross Fleet Street and turn left. On your right, you will pass:

13. The Wig and Pen Club, 229–230 The Strand. Begun in 1625, this famous fraternity is London's most exclusive private club for lawyers and journalists.

The monument in the center of The Strand is:

14. Temple Bar, a 20-foot tall obelisk marking the boundary between the City of London and the borough of Westminster. Topped by a bronze griffin or dragon and surrounded by statues of royalty (including Queen Victoria), the bar was erected in 1880 and is actually a memorial to two previous gates that occupied this spot for hundreds of years. The monument, and much of the surrounding area, is named for its proximity to Temple Church, which previously belonged to the order of the Knights Templar, a powerful religious brotherhood in the Middle Ages.

A few steps ahead, stop outside:

15. Child & Co., 1 Fleet Street, a private bank started by Francis Child in 1673. Child's Bank was the model for "Tellson's Bank," in Dickens's *A Tale of Two Cities.*

Continue half a block to the traffic light and look up. Above the gateway on your right is:

16. Prince Henry's Room, 17 Fleet Street, a fantastically preserved building that dates back to 1610; it is one of few
remaining wooden structures that survived London's Great Fire
of 1666.

Originally an inn called "The Princes Arms," the building
later housed Mrs. Salmon's Waxworks, a kind of early Madame
Tussaud's that became a favorite haunt of the young Charles
Dickens. In his book *David Copperfield,* Dickens's hero goes
"to see some perspiring wax works in Fleet Street" and mocks
the funny-looking, sweating figures.

Today Prince Henry's Room is a museum that focuses on the
17th-century diarist Samuel Pepys (for more information on
Pepys, see Stop 3 in "A Historical Pub Walk" tour). The staircase
to the left of the front gates will take you up to the small, yet
beautifully constructed, room. The thick, oak-paneled walls are
adorned with the three-feather emblem of the Prince of Wales,
while the initials of Prince Henry, who became Prince of Wales
in 1610, are set in plaster relief on the ceiling.

Continue a few steps farther along Fleet Street to:

17. Cock Tavern, 22 Fleet Street. Originally located across the
street in 1546, when it was known as the "Cock Ale House," the
tavern was moved to its present site in 1887. The Cock has a long
association with writers. The poet Alfred, Lord Tennyson
composed his "Will Waterproofs Lyrical Monologue" here. It
begins:

> *O plump head waiter at the Cock*
> *to which I most resort;*
> *How goes the time, 'tis five o'clock*
> *Go fetch a pint of port.*

The diarist Samuel Pepys came here, as did the lexicographer
Dr. Samuel Johnson, the actor David Garrick, and the playwright Oliver Goldsmith. The pub also has Dickensian associations because Dickens was a regular, and he actually made his
last public appearance here just one month before his death in
1870.

Return to Prince Henry's Room, cross Fleet Street, turn right
and, just past Chancery Lane, turn left into the narrow alleyway.
At the end of the alley, you'll see:

18. The Old Gates of Clifford's Inn. This 17th-century gatehouse is now all that remains of the Old Inn, which was a prep school for aspiring attorneys from the 15th through the 18th centuries. You may recall that in Dickens's novel *Little Dorrit,* Little Dorrit's brother, Tip, found "a stool and twelve shillings a week in the office of the attorney in Clifford's Inn and here languished for six months."

This was a rather unpleasant place in Dickens's day. In *Our Mutual Friend,* John Rokesmith, a principal character, meets Mr. Boffin on the street and says, " 'Would you object to turn aside into this place—I think it is called Clifford's Inn—where we can hear one another better than in the roaring street?' Mr. Boffin glanced into the mouldy little plantation, or cat-preserve, of Clifford's Inn as it was that day. . . . Sparrows were there, dry rot and wet rot were there but it was not otherwise a suggestive spot."

Return to Fleet Street, turn left, and continue two doors down to:

19. St. Dunstan's-in-the-West, Fleet Street, the octagonal church. The large clock on the church's tower was installed by the congregation to express its thanks that the building was spared from the Great Fire of 1666. However, the original church was totally replaced in the early 19th century. The present building, which dates from 1829–1833, is an excellent, early example of Gothic Revival architecture. The clock itself dates back to 1671; its two giant clubs still strike a reverberating bell every 15 minutes. This was the first clock in London with a double face and with minutes marked on its dial. Dickens mentioned the clock in both *Barnaby Rudge* and *David Copperfield.*

Inside the church you can see monuments to a swordsman and to an honest solicitor. Look for the Lord Mayor's sword from the Battle of Culloden, the battle that decisively defeated the Scottish uprising under Bonnie Prince Charlie in 1746. Also look for an icon screen brought here from Antim Monastery in Bucharest.

Continue several blocks along Fleet Street to the corner of:

20. Johnson's Court. Although nothing from Dickens's day survives on this street, the writer's career began here. Johnson's Court was once the address of *Monthly Magazine*'s office. John Forster wrote that Dickens "stealthily one evening at twilight" dropped off an article "with fear and trembling" that *Monthly Magazine* accepted. It became his first published piece. This, as well as other early works by Dickens, was published under the pseudonym "Boz," his younger brother's nickname.

Continue 2 blocks farther along Fleet Street and turn left into Wine Office Court. A few yards up on the right is:

REFUELING STOP   Ye Olde Cheshire Cheese, Wine Office Court, 145 Fleet Street (tel. 071/353-6170), one of the city's oldest pubs and one of Dickens's favorite watering holes. The pub's vaulted cellar may have been part of the Old Whitefriars Monastery that once occupied this site. There has been a tavern here since the 1590s. After it burned down in the Great Fire of 1666, Ye Olde Cheshire Cheese was quickly rebuilt, thus becoming the first pub to reopen after the fire. Downstairs, you can still see charred wooden beams that date back to that event.

Dickens's regular table, mentioned in *A Tale of Two Cities,* was to the right of the fireplace, opposite the bar in the ground floor room.

Earlier in this century the pub gained an additional measure of fame thanks to its foul-mouthed mascot, Polly the parrot. On Armistice Day 1918, the bird imitated the popping of a champagne cork 400 times and then fainted. Throughout the 1920s Polly was renowned for her ability to swear in several languages. Polly's death, in 1926, was announced on the BBC World Service, and the *London Times* carried her obituary under the headline "International Expert in Profanity Dies." Now stuffed and mounted and looking somewhat bedraggled, Polly can be seen inside a glass case above the ground floor bar.

Continue through Wine Office Court, bear left across the courtyard, and walk half a block into Gough (pronounced "Goff") Square to:

21. Dr. Johnson's House, 17 Gough Square (tel. 071/353-3745). A significant literary scholar and critic, Samuel Johnson (1709–1784) lived and worked here, compiling the world's first English-language dictionary. Johnson lived quite humbly. When the artist Joshua Reynolds visited Dr. Johnson's long attic, he observed that "besides his books, all covered with dust, there was an old crazy meal table, and still worse, an older elbow chair having only three legs." Johnson's house is now a museum of memorabilia; his original dictionary is on display. Admission is charged.

Exit Gough Square through the passageway opposite Dr. Johnson's House. Turn left onto Gunpowder Square, then straight to Printer Street. Turn right onto Little New Street, then left onto St. Andrew Street. Continue 5 blocks to Holborn Circus. The statue in the center of the road is of Queen Victoria's consort, Prince Albert. He is raising his hat to the City of London. On the corner to your right is:

22. St. Andrew Holborn, Holborn Circus, the largest Sir Christopher Wren–designed parish church. Upon his death in 1348, a local merchant, John Thane, willed all his houses and shops to this church; his bequest still provides for the church's upkeep to this day. St. Andrew is mentioned in *Oliver Twist,* when the burglar Bill Sykes looks up at the clock tower and says to Oliver, "Hard upon seven! You must step out." The two left from here and robbed a house.

There has been a succession of churches on this site since 951. The present building, which was damaged by air raids during World War II, was restored in 1961.

Turn left onto Holborn and walk 2 blocks where, just after the Midland Bank, you'll see the entrance to:

23. Barnard's Inn, a former prep school for students of the Inns of Court. It's confusing that so many buildings are called "inns," and apparently Dickens thought so too. In *Great Expectations* the protagonist, Pip, says of Barnard's, "I had supposed that establishment to be a hotel kept by Mr. Barnard. Whereas I now found Barnard to be a disembodied spirit, or a fiction, and his inn the dingiest collection of shabby buildings ever squeezed together in a rank corner as a club for Tom-cats."

Three blocks ahead on Holborn is:

24. Staple Inn, present-day headquarters of the Institute of Actuaries. The timber front of the Inn dates from 1576. It is London's last existing example of domestic architecture from Shakespeare's day. The Inn was originally a hostel for wool staplers, or brokers, and thus the name. Walk through the gates, where a sign on your left warns: "The porter has orders to prevent old clothes men and others from calling 'articles for sale' "—in other words, "No soliciting." Once inside, you'll find yourself in one of a few tranquil oases that even Dickens liked. As he wrote in *The Mystery of Edwin Drood:* "Behind the most ancient part of Holborn, London, where certain gabled houses some centuries of age still stand looking on the public way . . . is a little nook called Staple Inn. It is one of those nooks the turning into which out of the clashing streets, imparts to the relieved pedestrian the sensation of having put cotton in his ears and velvet soles on his boots. . . ." Pause and consider just how little this place has changed since Dickens wrote those sentences.

Cross the cobblestone courtyard under the passageway, noting the old water pump on your left. At the end of the passageway, look at the building immediately on your left. This is:

25. The Residence of Mr. Grewgious, the kindly lawyer in *The Mystery of Edwin Drood.* A stone above the door bears the inscription "PJT 1757." In the novel, Dickens wondered why Grewgious was not curious about what PJT might stand for, other than "perhaps John Thomas" or "probably Joe Tyler." In fact, the initials are those of the president of the inn, John Thompson.

Turn right, into the unmarked walkway, climb the steps, and turn right onto a road called Staple Inn Buildings. Walk 1 block, cross High Holborn, and turn left. Three blocks ahead is:

REFUELING STOP   Citte of York Pub, 22–23 High Holborn (tel. 071/242-7670). Even though it is one of the largest pubs around, this grand, Victorian-style tavern offers unparalleled intimacy in cozy cubicles. Once popular with lawyers who came here to speak confidentially with clients, the pub is now popular with office workers and other savvy patrons. There is a second bar in the cellar.

Exit the pub and immediately turn left down a small alley to:

26. Gray's Inn, another of London's four Inns of Court and one that certainly did not impress Dickens. In *The Uncommercial Traveller,* he wrote: "Indeed, I look upon Gray's Inn generally as one of the most depressing institutions in brick and mortar known to the children of men."

The passageway opens up into a part of the inn called:

27. South Square. In 1828, when Dickens was 16, he worked here as a clerk for the law firm Ellis and Blackmore (Number 1 South Square). Mischievously, the young author-to-be used to drop small stones from the upstairs windows onto the heads of unsuspecting lawyers below! Dickens learned shorthand here in the hope of becoming a newspaper reporter who would cover the House of Commons. Although Dickens's career goals changed, the shorthand he learned probably led to his phonetic style of writing.

The black statue on the far side of the lawn is of Sir Francis Bacon, Lord Chancellor of England under Elizabeth I. The statue was erected in 1912 and shows Bacon wearing his official robes. A writer, philosopher, and influential scientific theorist, his best known work is his *Essays,* remarkable for their pithy, epigrammatic style.

The church-like building at the far side of the square is:

28. Gray's Inn Hall. Built in 1556, the hall hosted the first performance of Shakespeare's *Comedy of Errors* in 1594. This square is mentioned in many of Dickens's books. In *The Pickwick Papers* "Clerk after clerk hastened into the square by one or other of the entrances, and looking up at the hall clock accelerated or decreased his rate of walking according to the time at which his office hours nominally commenced."

Exit South Square on the road that runs along the left side of Gray's Inn Hall and take the first left onto the pathway that runs under the buildings. Pass the gardens and take the first right onto Gray's Inn Place. After 4 blocks, turn right onto Theobald's Road, then take the first left onto John Street, which becomes Doughty Street. About 5 blocks ahead, on your right, you'll see:

29. Dickens's House, 48 Doughty Street (tel. 071/405-2127), the author's only surviving London home. Dickens moved here in 1837, before he was well known. While living here Dickens finished *The Pickwick Papers,* as well as *Oliver Twist* and *Nicholas Nickleby,* and started work on *Barnaby Rudge.* By the time Dickens left this house, in 1839, he was world famous. The author's letters, furniture, and first editions can be seen in glass display cases, adjacent to rooms that have been restored. There is an admission charge.

WALKING TOUR 3

A Historical Pub Walk

Start: Embankment Underground Station.
Finish: Covent Garden Market.
Time: 2½ hours, including pauses for refreshment.
Best Times: During pub hours: Monday through Saturday from 11am to 11pm and Sunday from noon to 3pm and 7 to 10:30pm. If you take your walk around lunch time, you can sample traditional "pub grub." After 5pm, or around sunset, is a good time to drink with the locals.
Worst Times: Late night, when the streets are dark, and on Sunday, when pubs keep shorter hours and other sights are closed.

There is nothing more British than a pub. The public house is exactly that—the British public's place to meet, exchange stories, tell jokes, and drink. Many efforts have been made to create something resembling a pub outside Britain, but they do not capture the unique feel of the real McCoy. Pubs are almost as old as England itself. In the 12th century, a local wit noted that there were two plagues in London: fire and drink. In an earlier era, the Royal Navy's rations included one gallon of ale per man per day. An occasional afternoon or, more often, an evening spent in a pub is part of British social life. And on Sunday afternoon, entire families often go to the pub for lunch. (Note, however, that children under 14 are not allowed in pubs at all, and no one under 18 may legally be served alcohol.)

Beer is the principal drink sold in pubs; don't even try to order a martini. Available in imperial half-pints and pints (20% larger than U.S. measures), the choice is usually between lager and bitter, and the locals usually opt for the latter. Many pubs serve particularly good "real" ales, which can be distinguished at the bar by handpumps that must be "pulled" by the barkeep. Real ales are natural "live" beers that have been allowed to ferment in the cask. Unlike lagers, English ales are served at room temperature and may take some getting used to. For an unusual and tasty alternative, try cider, a flavorful fermented apple juice that's so good you'll hardly notice the alcohol—until later.

As a rule, there is no table service in pubs; drinks (and food) must be ordered at the bar. Tipping at a pub is not customary; it should be reserved for exemplary service.

Pubs used to be required to close in the afternoons, but a 1988 change in the law—which most people toasted—now allows pubs to stay open from 11am to 11pm Monday through Saturday and from noon to 3pm and 7 to 10:30pm on Sunday. Not all pubs have taken advantage of this new freedom, however; some still close daily between 3 and 7pm.

Carpeted floors, etched glass, and carved-wood bars are the hallmarks of most pubs. But each one looks different, and each has its own special atmosphere and clientele. Greater London's 5,000-plus pubs mean that you'll never have to walk more than a couple of blocks to find one, and part of the enjoyment of "pubbing" is discovering a special one on your own. This tour will take you to some of the most famous, as well as some of the least-known, watering holes in the city—an excellent cross section of taverns united by their historical uniqueness. Enjoy!

Take the left exit from Embankment Underground Station and walk up Villiers Street. Don't walk too far, though. The first brown wooden door on your right is the entrance to:

1. **Gordon's,** 47 Villiers Street (tel. 071/930-1408). Although not a pub, it is the most atmospheric and eccentric wine bar you'll ever visit. Wine bars are a relatively recent phenomenon in London, offering an excellent alternative to the traditional pub. Most have a good selection by the glass or the bottle, and food is almost always served. The menus tend to have a continental

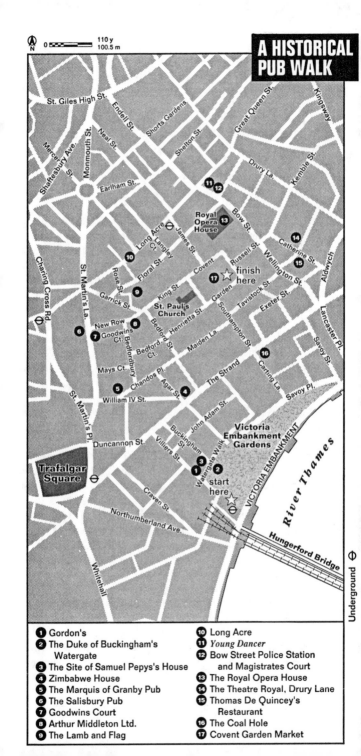

A HISTORICAL PUB WALK

0 ___ 110 y
0 ___ 100.5 m

Trafalgar Square

Royal Opera House

St. Paul's Church

Covent Garden

Victoria Embankment Gardens

River Thames

Hungerford Bridge

finish here

start here

Underground

1. Gordon's
2. The Duke of Buckingham's Watergate
3. The Site of Samuel Pepys's House
4. Zimbabwe House
5. The Marquis of Granby Pub
6. The Salisbury Pub
7. Goodwins Court
8. Arthur Middleton Ltd.
9. The Lamb and Flag
10. Long Acre
11. *Young Dancer*
12. Bow Street Police Station and Magistrates Court
13. The Royal Opera House
14. The Theatre Royal, Drury Lane
15. Thomas De Quincey's Restaurant
16. The Coal Hole
17. Covent Garden Market

emphasis, with standards and prices that are higher than at most pubs. You don't have to eat, however; in fact, a bottle of the house wine shared among two or three people may be less expensive than visiting a pub.

At Gordon's, yellowed newspapers adorn the walls; model Spitfires, covered in dust, hang from the ceiling; and rickety tables crowd the floor. The bar's cozy, candlelit drinking room features intimately low ceilings. Gordon's unusual decor and atmosphere make it an important stop on this tour. Gordon's is not open on Saturday or Sunday.

Leaving Gordon's, turn left onto Villiers Street and immediately left again down the steps to Watergate Walk. Walk along the pathway where, 1 block ahead on your right, is:

2. The Duke of Buckingham's Watergate. Before the 1862 construction of the Victoria Embankment (which keeps the Thames in check), this stone gateway marked the river's high-tide line and protected the duke's mansion (which once stood behind it). The inscription on top the gate reads "Fidei Coticula Crux" ("The cross is the touchstone of faith")—the duke's family motto. After the mansion was demolished in 1675, the grounds were turned into a public park. These are the gardens George Orwell wrote about in *Down and Out in Paris and London* and the place where Orwell slept while living as a vagrant in the 1930s.

With your back to the watergate, climb the flight of stone steps, walk through the iron gate, and enter Buckingham Street. On your left is:

3. The Site of Samuel Pepys's (1633–1703) House, 14 Buckingham Street. Despite a long and distinguished career as an official in naval affairs, Pepys (pronounced "Peeps") is best remembered for the detailed diary he kept from 1660 to 1669. Thanks to this diary we know more about Pepys than about any other person of his time. Candidly honest, Pepys concealed the contents of his diary from his wife by using his own personal code—a complex mix of foreign and invented words. Pepys's diary is not only an important history of the events and manners of his day, but it is a fascinating psychological study of Pepys himself. As with most diaries, reading this one often seems voyeuristic. After being caught in a liaison with his maid, Pepys wrote that his wife pulled aside the bed curtain and with red hot tongs "made as if she did design to pinch me with them." Most of Pepys's entries were written at night by candlelight, a practice that eventually ruined his eyesight. The diarist moved from this house in 1701, two years before his death.

Walk up Buckingham Street, cross John Adam Street, climb

the steps, and walk through Buckingham Arcade to The Strand. Cross at the crosswalk, turn right on The Strand, and at the corner of Agar Street look across the street at:

4. **Zimbabwe House,** the present location of the Zimbabwe High Commission. Look up at the second-story windows, between which stand nude statues depicting the Ages of Man. The unclad figures caused such an outcry when they were unveiled by the sculptor Jacob Epstein in 1908 that the windows of the building across the street were replaced with frosted glass to obscure the view. After the Southern Rhodesian High Commission moved into the building in the 1930s, one of the statue's "private" parts broke off and almost struck a pedestrian below. Orders were given to "remove the protruding parts" of the statues, which is why none of them now has a "head"!

With your back to Zimbabwe House, turn left onto William IV Street, then right into Chandos Place. On the corner is:

5. **The Marquis of Granby Pub,** 51 Chandos Place (tel. 071/836-7657). This tavern dates from the reign of Charles II, when it was known as "The Hole in the Wall," and run by an ex-mistress of the second Duke of Buckingham. In the 19th century, Claude Duval, one of England's most notorious robbers and a consummate ladies man, was arrested while drinking here. After his trial and execution, Duval was buried under a tombstone that reads:

> *Here lies Duval.*
> *Reader: if male, thou art look to thy purse*
> *If female, to thy heart.*

The pub was renamed in the late 18th century in honor of General John Manners, the Marquis of Granby, who led the English army in 1759 at the Battle of Minden during the Seven Years War that resulted in a victory over the French. Today, this cheerful tavern's old-fashioned English-inn atmosphere makes it popular with actors and workers from the nearby theaters. It's especially busy at lunchtime.

Exit the pub, walk 1 block down Chandos Place, and turn left again onto Bedfordbury. One block ahead, turn left onto Mays Court, then right, onto St. Martin's Lane. Diagonally across the street from the Lumiere Cinema (which is now owned by former Beatle George Harrison) on your left, you will come to:

6. **The Salisbury Pub,** 90 St. Martin's Lane (tel. 071/836-5863). Formerly known as the "Coach and Horses" and later as "Ben Caunts's Head," this 1852 tavern gained fame for the bare-

knuckle prize fights that used to take place here. Beautifully preserved, the pub's magnificent marble fittings, cut-glass mirrors, brass statuettes, plush seats, and art-nouveau decor make it one of the most attractive in London. The quintessential theater pub, the Salisbury touts itself as the "archetype of actors' pubs, and as much a part of the world of the stage as greasepaint." This may be true, since the glittering Edwardian tavern has long been a famous meeting place for theatrical folk.

As you leave the Salisbury, cross St. Martin's Lane; almost directly ahead, climb the two steps at 55–56 St. Martin's Lane to enter:

7. Goodwins Court, an almost secret, terrifically preserved 18th-century street. At night, the bucolic gas-lamp-lit court looks like a perfectly manicured Hollywood set. It's pure magic.

Walk through Goodwins Court and turn left on Bedfordbury. On the corner of New Row is:

8. Arthur Middleton Ltd., 12 New Row, purveyors of antique scientific tools and instruments. Take a look inside; you might find centuries-old telescopes, weather data devices, and surgical instruments. The window displays are usually pretty good, too.

Turn right onto New Row, cross Garrick Street, and continue straight ahead onto Rose Street to:

9. The Lamb and Flag, 33 Rose Street (tel. 071/497-9504). Built in 1623, this is one of the few wood-frame structures in central London to survive the Great Fire of 1666. A favorite haunt of Charles Dickens, this pub was once known as the "Bucket of Blood" because of the many fights that broke out here. The poet John Dryden (1631–1700) was attacked and beaten in the side alley, allegedly by thugs hired by the Earl of Rochester, who was unhappy about a vicious lampoon that Dryden had written. The anniversary of the December 16th attack is marked each year when The Lamb and Flag holds a festive "Dryden Night."

Leave the pub through the wood-lined alleyway and turn right, onto Floral Street. After about 300 yards, turn left onto Langley Court, then right onto:

10. Long Acre, Covent Garden's main thoroughfare and a popular shopping street. Built on a sloping hill, Long Acre connects Covent Garden with Leicester Square. At night, especially on weekends, this is one of the busiest streets in London.

Walk about 6 blocks, passing the Covent Garden Underground Station, turn right onto Bow Street, and walk 1 block to see:

11. Young Dancer, a beautiful statue by Enzo Plazzotta (1921–1981). London is jam packed with outdoor statues—some 1,700 at last count—but most are old memorials to even older statesmen. *Young Dancer* is one of the few examples in London of good modern outdoor sculpture. This statue is to honor dancers of the Royal Ballet who perform at the Royal Opera House, located just steps away.

Next to the statue on the corner is:

12. Bow Street Police Station and Magistrates Court. Henry Fielding, author of *The History of Tom Jones,* became a Justice of the Peace in 1747 and ran his court at Number 4 Bow Street (now demolished). Along with his blind half brother, John, Fielding helped establish the Bow Street Runners, London's first salaried, permanent police force.

Opposite the Police Station is:

13. The Royal Opera House (tel. 071/240-1066), home to both the Royal Opera and the Royal Ballet companies. Opened in 1858, the posh theater was designed by E. M. Barry (who also designed the adjoining cast-iron and glass Floral Hall). Unless Pavarotti is scheduled to sing, you can often get tickets on the day of the opera. While good seats are predictably expensive, upper-level benches usually cost less than a movie, but they are rather far from the stage.

Continue down Bow Street, turn left onto Russell Street, then immediately right onto Catherine Street to:

14. The Theatre Royal, Drury Lane, Catherine Street (tel. 071/836-8108), one of the oldest theaters in London. It was opened under a royal charter in 1663 by the playwright and Poet Laureate Thomas Killigrew (who is widely believed to be the illegitimate son of Shakespeare). Killigrew also made theatrical history by hiring the first female actress to perform professionally on the English stage.

In 1742 David Garrick, one of the city's most famous actors, also made his debut here. Five years later he became the Theatre Royal's manager; in this capacity, he staged numerous Shakespearean revivals. The theater changed hands in 1777, when it was taken over by Richard Brinsley Sheridan. Unfortunately, the building was not insured, and when the theater caught fire in 1809, all Sheridan could do was sit down with a glass of port and watch the blaze, commenting "Surely a man may take a glass of wine by his own fireside." The present building, which dates from 1812, is modeled after the great theater at Bordeaux. Major musicals are usually staged here.

Continue down Catherine Street and turn right on Tavistock Street. Across the road is:

15. Thomas de Quincey's Restaurant, 36 Tavistock Street (tel. 071/240-3773), located in the former home of Thomas de

Quincey (1785–1859), author of *Confessions of an English Opium Eater*. When De Quincey was a young man, he started taking opium to numb the effects of a painful gastric disease. Before long De Quincey became heavily addicted and, for most of his life, was just barely able to support his family by writing newspaper and magazine articles. As an old man, he became a celebrated eccentric—alone and poverty stricken.

Just a few steps ahead, turn left onto Wellington Street. Walk down the hill, cross Exeter Street, and go through the portico of the Lyceum Theater. Turn right on The Strand, cross to the south side of the street, and continue 2 blocks to:

16. The Coal Hole, 91 The Strand (tel. 071/836-7503), one of Central London's largest pubs. It was established in the early 19th century for the coal haulers who unloaded boats on the River Thames. Like many other pubs in and around the West End, The Coal Hole has numerous theatrical connections. In the mid-19th century, the actor Edmund Kean would hire gangs of rowdies and get them drunk here before sending them to the Drury Lane's rival theaters to heckle the actors and cause trouble. Look for an inscription on one of the pub's interior wooden beams commemorating The Wolf Club, an informal group organized by Kean for men whose wives didn't allow them to sing in the bath!

Cross The Strand and continue straight ahead to Southampton Street. Walk up the hill to:

17. Covent Garden Market, a covered mall packed with interesting shops, sidewalk cafés, street performers, and tourists. Originally designed in the 1630s by Inigo Jones, one of London's most famous architects, this was a residential square that eventually fell into disrepair. Only Jones's St. Paul's Church remains, located on the west side of the square. Named for a centuries-old convent that once stood here, the Covent Garden Market housed a flower market from 1860 until 1974, when it was removed to Nine Elms. The modern shopping and nightlife center that now occupies this space is a flourishing center for restaurants, cafés, bars, and, of course, pubs. The three pubs on the north side of the market (toward Covent Garden Underground Station) are all top picks for cozy comfort and lively atmosphere (as well as above-average pub grub). Any one of these would make a fine choice for ending your historical walk. Cheers!

WALKING TOUR 4

Westminster & Whitehall

Start: Trafalgar Square.
Finish: Parliament Square.
Time: 1½ hours, not including museum stops.
Best Times: When the museums are open, Monday through Saturday from 10am to 5:30pm, and Sunday from 2 to 5:30pm.
Worst Times: Early Sunday, when the museums are closed.

Whitehall, a single, long thoroughfare that connects Trafalgar Square with Parliament Square, is the center of government. The entire length of the thoroughfare was once fronted by the old Palace of Whitehall until it burned down in 1698. Today, both the home and foreign offices have a Whitehall address, as do a host of other government departments. The official residence of the prime minister is just steps away, on Downing Street, and the spectacular Houses of Parliament are at the end of the block, towering over Parliament Square.

This walking tour will parallel the River Thames and take you past some of London's most famous buildings and monuments of historical and contemporary interest.

Start your tour at Trafalgar Square, which can be reached by taking the tube to the Charing Cross or Embankment Underground stations (within 1 block of each other). Be careful of traffic as you cross to the center of:

1. **Trafalgar Square,** often considered to be the heart of London. To the east of the square is the City, London's financial center. To the north are Leicester Square and the commercial West End, London's entertainment and shopping areas. To the west is The Mall, the royal road that leads to Buckingham Palace. And to the south is Whitehall, the nation's seat of government. At the center of Trafalgar Square is:

2. **Nelson's Column,** one of the most famous monuments in London, commemorating Viscount Horatio Nelson's victory over a French and Spanish fleet at the Battle of Trafalgar (1805). The column is topped with a statue of Lord Nelson. The granite statue itself stands 17 feet high. It is so heavy it had to be hoisted up in three different sections. At the base of the column are the famous:

3. **Bronze Lions and Trafalgar Fountains.** The entire square is the site of London's large annual New Year's Eve party. Of the three other sculptures in Trafalgar Square, the most interesting is:

4. **The Equestrian Statue of George IV** that was originally intended to top Marble Arch (now located at the northeast corner of Hyde Park). One wonders why the king rides without boots on a horse without stirrups or saddle.

Leave the square on the north side (again, be careful of fast-moving traffic) and walk to:

5. **The National Gallery** (tel. 071/839-3321), an imposing building that houses Britain's finest collection of paintings by such world-class masters as Rembrandt, Raphael, Botticelli, Goya, and Hogarth. The gallery's permanent collection, arranged by school, includes representative works from almost every major 13th- to 20th-century European artist. Temporary displays include selected works from the museum's own collection, as well as some of the world's top traveling exhibits.

Works by such 19th-century French painters as Monet, Renoir, and Cézanne are especially popular. In the lower-floor galleries, one can see damaged paintings by great artists as well as excellent forgeries.

Call ahead to take advantage of one of the regularly scheduled guided tours or guest lecturers. The gallery offers special brochures, books, and educational events to focus attention on various aspects of its truly remarkable collection.

The gallery's main entrance is flanked by two great statues. On the left is:

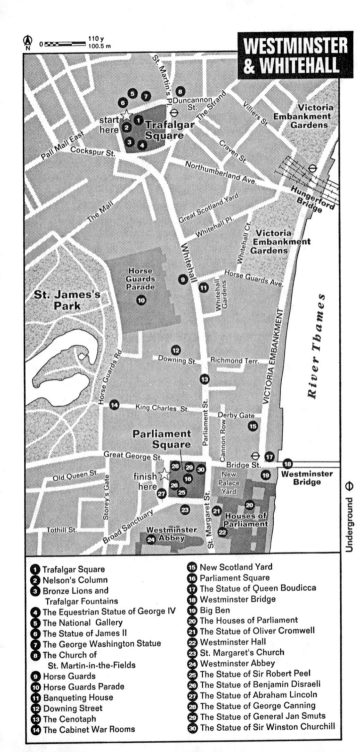

0 — 110 y / 100.5 m

N

St. Martin's Pl.
Duncannon St.
The Strand
Villiers St.

Victoria Embankment Gardens

start here
Trafalgar Square

Pall Mall East
Cockspur St.
Craven St.

Northumberland Ave.

Hungerford Bridge

The Mall

Great Scotland Yard
Whitehall Pl.

Victoria Embankment Gardens

St. James's Park

Horse Guards Parade

Whitehall

Horse Guards Ave.

Whitehall Gardens
Whitehall Ct.

Horse Guards Rd

Downing St.
Richmond Terr.

River Thames

King Charles St.
Parliament St.
Derby Gate

Old Queen St.

Parliament Square

Great George St.

finish here

Cannon Row

Storey's Gate

Bridge St.

Westminster Bridge

Tothill St.

Broad Sanctuary

St. Margaret St.

New Palace Yard

Houses of Parliament

Westminster Abbey

Underground

1 Trafalgar Square
2 Nelson's Column
3 Bronze Lions and Trafalgar Fountains
4 The Equestrian Statue of George IV
5 The National Gallery
6 The Statue of James II
7 The George Washington Statue
8 The Church of St. Martin-in-the-Fields
9 Horse Guards
10 Horse Guards Parade
11 Banqueting House
12 Downing Street
13 The Cenotaph
14 The Cabinet War Rooms
15 New Scotland Yard
16 Parliament Square
17 The Statue of Queen Boudicca
18 Westminster Bridge
19 Big Ben
20 The Houses of Parliament
21 The Statue of Oliver Cromwell
22 Westminster Hall
23 St. Margaret's Church
24 Westminster Abbey
25 The Statue of Sir Robert Peel
26 The Statue of Benjamin Disraeli
27 The Statue of Abraham Lincoln
28 The Statue of George Canning
29 The Statue of General Jan Smuts
30 The Statue of Sir Winston Churchill

6. **The Statue of James II,** a work created in 1686 by Grinling Gibbons, one of England's noted sculptors. The statue is widely regarded as one of the country's finest. James II ascended the throne in 1685 and quickly levied new—and unpopular—taxes. The king might have succeeded if he had not been so determined to restore Catholicism to England—a move that led to his deposition and forced exile in France, where he remained for the rest of his life. After James II died (1701), Benedictine monks kept his body embalmed in a French hearse for 92 years, waiting until the political and religious climate in England would change enough so that the former king could be buried in his native land. This never came to pass, however, and so James II was eventually buried at St. Germain.

On the right side of the gallery's entrance is:

7. **The George Washington Statue,** a gift from the state of Virginia—a replica of the statue located in the state capitol building in Richmond.

Walk clockwise around Trafalgar Square to:

8. **The Church of St. Martin-in-the-Fields** (tel. 071/930-1862), located on the northeastern corner of the square. This popular London church is famous for its spire-topped classical portico—a style often copied in 18th-century America. Begun in 1722, the church is the burial site of several famous people, including the furniture designer Thomas Chippendale, and painters William Hogarth and Sir Joshua Reynolds. After visiting the church, go downstairs to the London Brass Rubbing Centre where, for a small fee, you will be provided with materials and instructions for making rubbings of replicas of medieval church brasses.

On Monday and Tuesday at 1pm, the church usually holds free chamber-music concerts, often featuring works by well-known 19th-century composers. St. Martin's is also known for its exceptional choir; consider attending a full choral Sunday service.

The church is open to visitors Monday through Saturday from 10am to 6pm, Sunday from noon to 6pm.

Continue clockwise around the square and exit Trafalgar Square via Whitehall.

REFUELING STOP   If you're ready for a light snack or a pint, turn left at the second street off Whitehall—Great Scotland Yard. Cross Northumberland Avenue to **The Sherlock Holmes Pub,** 10 Northumberland Street (tel. 071/930-2644). In the upstairs dining room of this popular "theme" pub, you'll find a re-creation of Holmes's fictional living room at 221b Baker Street. The head of the Hound of the Baskervilles (from the book of the same name) and other mementoes decorate the downstairs bar.

Back on Whitehall, continue for 1 block where, on your right, you will see two brightly suited guards on horseback. You have arrived at:

9. Horse Guards, home of the queen's ceremonial guards. The well-dressed mounted troopers are posted here daily from 10am to 4pm. There is a small, usually uncrowded, changing-of-the-guard ceremony here Monday through Saturday at 11am, Sunday at 10am. The most interesting event is probably the guard dismount, which takes place daily at 4pm.

Walk through the courtyard of Horse Guards and under the building's lofty Palladian-style arch. The park on the other side of the arch is called:

10. Horse Guards Parade—the site of the Trooping of the Colour, an impressive annual ceremony celebrating the queen's official birthday.

Return to Whitehall and cross to the other side of the street. The building at the corner of Horseguards Avenue is:

11. Banqueting House, the only remaining portion of the former Whitehall Palace. Modeled on Sansovino's Library in Venice, it was completed by Inigo Jones in 1622. The first purely Renaissance building in London, Banqueting House was intended for receptions, banquets, and theatrical performances. In 1635, King Charles I commissioned Peter Paul Rubens to paint the Banqueting House's ceilings, which glorified aspects of King Charles I's reign. Ironically, on January 30, 1649, that same king was brought here to be executed. Charles I stepped out of an upstairs window onto a waiting scaffold and, in a steady voice, said, "I needed not have come here, and therefore I tell you (and I pray God it be not laid to your charge) that I am the martyr of the people." The king then placed his long hair under his cap, laid his neck on the chopping block, and stretched out his hands as a signal to the executioner to strike. His head was severed in a single blow, then held up to the crowds below, with the words "behold the head of a traitor."

The light-brown, brick building next to Banqueting House is the Welsh Office. The large building with the green roof, next door, is the Ministry of Defence.

Cross Whitehall again and walk 1 block to the iron gates on the right side. This is:

12. Downing Street, the address of the official residence of the British prime minister. Unlike most of the large government buildings on Whitehall, which were erected in the 19th century, Downing Street is small in scale, lined with homes dating from 1680 to 1766. The street is named after Sir George Downing, a 17th-century Member of Parliament and real estate developer. Downing built this cul-de-sac of plain brick terrace houses around 1680; the only remaining houses are Nos. 10, 11, and 12. No. 10, on the right side, has been home to prime ministers since 1732, when it was acquired by the Crown and offered as a personal gift to the First Lord of the Treasury, Sir Robert Walpole, who would only accept it as an office. No. 11 Downing Street is the office and home of the Chancellor of the Exchequer. Extensive alterations were made to both buildings in the 1950s and 1960s. Although they look small, these buildings actually have sizable rooms and offices.

The obelisk in the middle of Whitehall, just past Downing Street is:

13. The Cenotaph, a tall, white memorial to the dead of both World Wars. Often surrounded by flowers and wreaths, the monument of Portland stone was designed by Sir Edwin Lutyens and placed here in 1920. The word "cenotaph" derives from Greek words *kenos,* meaning empty, and *taphos,* meaning tomb. The monument's lines alternate between being slightly convex and concave, representing infinity. There are no religious symbols in the design; the only symbols are the flags of the three branches of the military, and the standard of the merchant fleet.

Half a block ahead, turn right onto King Charles Street and walk 1 block to:

14. The Cabinet War Rooms, the British government's underground World War II headquarters. Inside, you can see the Cabinet Room, Map Room, Prime Minister Winston Churchill's emergency bedroom, and the Telephone Room (where calls to Franklin D. Roosevelt were made). They have all been restored to their original 1940s' appearance—so accurately restored that there's even an open pack of cigarettes on the table. The rooms are open daily from 10am to 5:30pm. There is an admission charge.

Return to Whitehall, and cross the street to:

REFUELING STOP   The Red Lion Public House, 48 Parliament Street (tel. 071/930-5826), which is frequented by Members of Parliament and other civil servants. In fact, so many MPs come here that the pub sounds a "divisional bell" to call the lawmakers back to the Houses of Parliament before a vote is taken. The food is above average and the usual beers are available.

A few steps past the Red Lion, turn left onto Derby Gate and look down the road at the red brick buildings of:

15. New Scotland Yard, the former home of England's top police force. When the foundation stone was laid in 1875, the intention was to build a lofty national opera house. A shortage of money stopped the project midway through until 1878, when the police proposed converting the partially built structure into headquarters for their "A" division. Interestingly, the granite used for the new building was quarried by convicts from Dartmoor Prison. Described by the architect Norman Shaw as "a very constabulary kind of castle," the finished structure provided 140 offices for the elite group. Since there were no elevators, senior officers were assigned rooms on the lower floors, while lower-ranking policemen had the higher floors. In 1967, Scotland Yard left this building in favor of new headquarters on Victoria Street.

One block ahead you enter:

16. Parliament Square. Laid out in the 1860s by Charles Barry, who also designed the new Houses of Parliament, the square was remodeled earlier in this century when the center of the square was turned into a traffic island.

Turn left on Parliament Square and walk to the foot of Westminster Bridge. On your left, you will see:

17. The Statue of Queen Boudicca, depicting the ancient British queen (died A.D. 60) and her daughters in a war chariot. The sculpture was created by Thomas Hornicroft in the 1850s and unveiled here in 1902. It is believed that Prince Albert lent his horses as models for this statue.

Walk to the center of:

18. Westminster Bridge, a seven-arch, cast-iron span that opened in 1750, and was rebuilt in 1862. The bridge's 84-foot width was considered exceptionally large at that time.

From the center of the bridge, look left, toward the City of London. It was this view that, in 1802, inspired William Wordsworth to write:

> *Earth has not anything to show more fair:*
> *Dull would he be of soul who could pass by*

> *A sight so touching in its majesty:*
> *This City now doth like a garment wear*
> *The beauty of the morning; silent, bare,*
> *Ships, towers, domes, theatres, and temples lie*
> *Open unto the fields, and to the sky;*
> *All bright and glittering in the smokeless air. . . .*
> —"Upon Westminster Bridge"

Admittedly, the view from the bridge has changed considerably since Wordsworth's day, though there are still some wonderful sights. From Westminster Bridge, you can see the ornate back side of the Houses of Parliament. The balcony with the green canopy is the river terrace of the House of Commons; the one with the red canopy is the river terrace of the House of Lords.

Return toward Parliament Square and stand at the foot of:

19. Big Ben, the most famous clock tower in the world. Contrary to popular belief, Big Ben doesn't refer either to the tower or to the clock; it is the name of the largest bell in the chime. Hung in 1856, the bell may have been named for either Sir Benjamin Hall (the commissioner of works when the bell was hung) or Ben Caunt (a popular prize fighter of that era who, at age 42, fought in a match that lasted 60 rounds). The tower's four huge, 200-foot-high clocks each has a minute hand as large as a double-decker bus.

Stroll past the front of:

20. The Houses of Parliament, home of England's national legislature—which is made up of the House of Commons and House of Lords. Officially known as the Royal Palace of St. Stephen at Westminster, the Houses are located on the site of a royal palace built by King Edward the Confessor before the Norman Conquest of 1066. During Edward's reign, this stretch of land along the Thames was surrounded by water and known as "Thorny Island" due to the wild brambles that flourished there. The island had become sort of a pilgrimage site, celebrated for several miracles believed to have taken place there. When Edward ascended the throne, he chose this sacred spot to build both the royal palace and royal church (Westminster Abbey). Later kings improved and enlarged the palace, which served as the official royal residence until 1512, when it was destroyed by fire.

The present Gothic-style building, which contains more than 1,000 rooms and 2 miles of corridors, was designed by Charles Barry and Augustus Pugin and completed in 1860. On May 10, 1941, the House of Commons was destroyed by German bombs. It was rebuilt by Giles Gilbert Scott, the man who designed London's red telephone booths. Still, the House of Commons remains small. Only 346 of its 650 members can sit at any one time, while the rest crowd around the door and the Speaker's Chair. The ruling party and the opposition sit facing one another, two sword lengths apart. The House of Commons holds the political power in Parliament. The powers of the House of Lords were greatly curtailed in 1911. Unlike the Commons, whose members are elected, most of the members of the House of Lords are hereditary peers who inherit their parliamentary seats. The Lords' opulently furnished chambers have an almost sacrosanct feel. Debates here are not as interesting or lively as those in the more important House of Commons, but the visitors' waiting line is usually shorter; a visit here will help you appreciate the pageantry of Parliament.

Visitors may watch parliamentary debates from the Strangers' Galleries of Parliament's two houses. This can be most interesting and is especially exciting during debates on particularly controversial topics.

The House of Commons is usually open to the public Monday through Thursday beginning at 4pm and Friday from 9:30am to 3pm. The House of Lords is usually open Monday through Thursday beginning about 3pm and on certain Fridays. Line up at St. Stephen's Entrance, just past the statue of Oliver Cromwell (see below). The debates usually continue into the evening, but the lines become shorter after 6pm.

In the small garden, in front of the Houses of Parliament, you will see:

21. The Statue of Oliver Cromwell, a monument to England's first and only Lord Protector. Cromwell (1599–1658), who led the parliamentary armies during the Civil War that toppled King Charles I, is depicted here with a Bible in one hand and a sword in the other. When the statue was unveiled in 1899, it was vehemently criticized by Parliament's Irish representatives. Cromwell was hated in Ireland for his harsh policies, particularly the massacre of more than 30,000 men, women, and children in Drogheda, followed by a trail of death and devastation from Wexford to Connaught. Motivated by religious as well as political considerations, he awarded vast tracts of land to his loyal followers, leaving less than one-ninth of Irish soil in Irish hands. Ultimately, Parliament refused to pay for the statue, and the Prime Minister at that time, Lord Rosebery, eventually paid for it himself. Do Cromwell's eyes appear to be downcast, as though ashamed of something? Look across the street, directly opposite the statue. Above the small doorway of the church is a small bust of King Charles I, the monarch who was beheaded at Cromwell's instigation.

Directly behind the statue of Oliver Cromwell is:

22. Westminster Hall, the last remaining section of the old Houses of Parliament. A majestic vestige of Romanesque and Gothic architecture, the hall was built by William Rufus (ca. 1056–1100), the son of William the Conqueror. Something of a boaster, William Rufus once referred to this hall as nothing—a mere bed chamber to his future projects—but there were to be no more.

Rebuilt in 1394–1402 for Richard II, the hall is not much more than a large, rectangular banquet room, but it is noted for its magnificent oak hammerbeam roof. In the 14th century, Westminster Hall became a place where some of the highest courts witnessed famous trials, such as those of Anne Boleyn, Sir Thomas More, and Guy Fawkes, who conspired to blow up King James I and the Houses of Parliament in the Gunpowder Plot. The 1649 trial of King Charles I also took place here, before an extremely reluctant panel of judges. Despite the fact that he refused to accept the legality of this court, the king was found guilty; his sentence read: "for all which treasons and crimes this Court doth adjudge that sets as a tyrant, traitor, murderer, and publique enemy to the good people of this nations shall be put to death by the severing of his head from his body."

Oliver Cromwell was proclaimed Lord Protector here (his statue is outside); more recently, this is where Sir Winston Churchill's body lay in state. Since the criminal courts moved to the Royal Courts of Justice in the late 19th century, Westminster Hall is now used only occasionally, primarily as a private banquet hall for parliamentary functions. After a bomb killed an MP in 1979, entrance to Westminster Hall has become difficult. Tickets are available, on a limited basis, from your embassy.

Return to Parliament Square and cross St. Margaret Street to:

23. St. Margaret's Westminster, a grand 16th-century church that's often initially mistaken for Westminster Abbey. Since 1614 St. Margaret's has been the parish church of the House of Commons, but may be best known for its enormous, beautiful East Window, a stained-glass masterpiece presented to King Henry VII by Ferdinand and Isabella of Spain to commemorate the marriage of their daughter Catherine of Aragon to his eldest son, Prince Arthur.

Enter the church through the south door and look to your

right where, almost hidden from view, is a commemorative plaque to Sir Walter Raleigh, who is buried on these grounds. The diarist Samuel Pepys, and the poet John Milton are among several other famous Londoners interred here. (Pepys was also married here, as was Sir Winston Churchill.)

On bright days, the East Window is brilliantly illuminated. The stained-glass gift was originally intended for Westminster Abbey. But by the time it arrived here from Spain, Arthur had died and his brother Henry VIII had already married Catherine.

Exit St. Margaret's and walk a few steps to:

24. Westminster Abbey (tel. 071/222-5152). The Benedictine abbey, which housed a community of monks as early as A.D. 750, was called Westminster (West Monastery) because of its location west of the City of London. In 1052, Edward the Confessor initiated construction of the present building and it was consecrated in 1065. William the Conqueror was crowned at the Abbey in 1066, and most British monarchs have continued to be crowned there. Many have also been married and buried in the Abbey as well.

When not in use, the Coronation Chair (built in 1300) sits behind the Abbey's High Altar. Incorporated into the chair is the Stone of Scone, Scotland's coronation stone, which was taken from Scotland and brought to England in 1297 by King Edward I. The Stone has been retrieved and returned to Scotland by Scottish nationalists several times (most recently in the 1950s) but each time found its way back to London.

The Poet's Corner is the final resting place of some of Britain's most famous bards, including Geoffrey Chaucer, Robert Browning, and Lord Tennyson.

The Abbey's Henry VII Chapel, with its architectural extravagances and exquisite carvings, will take your breath away. Comprehensive "Super Tours" condense the Abbey's 900-year history into 1½ hours; although these tours are expensive, many people believe they are worth it.

The Abbey is open Monday through Saturday from 9am to 5pm. The Royal Chapels are open Monday, Tuesday, Thursday, and Friday from 9am to 4:45pm; Wednesday from 9am to 8pm; and Saturday from 9am to 2pm and 3:30 to 5:45pm. Entrance to the Abbey is free, but there is an admission charge to the Chapels (except Wednesday, the only time that photographs may be taken).

Exit Westminster Abbey and continue walking clockwise around Parliament Square. No doubt, you have noticed that the square is surrounded by statues—the greatest concentration of outdoor sculptures in the city. Cross Broad Sanctuary, to the west side of Parliament Square. On your right is:

25. The Statue of Sir Robert Peel, former Prime Minister and founder of London's Metropolitan Police Force. The statue, erected in 1876, depicts Peel wearing a frock coat.

On your right is:

26. The Statue of Benjamin Disraeli, England's first Prime Minister of Jewish ancestry. Standing with his back toward you, the statue was unveiled in 1883, on the second anniversary of Disraeli's death.

On your left is:

27. The Statue of Abraham Lincoln, the only non-British individual represented on the square. The monument, a gift from the city of Chicago, is an exact replica of the one in Lincoln Park.

The last sculpture on this side of the square is:

28. The Statue of George Canning. He was foreign secretary during the Napoleonic Wars and became prime minister in 1827. Reportedly, the figure fell over in the sculptor's studio and killed someone.

Continue walking to the north side of Parliament Square, where you will see:

29. The Statue of General Jan Smuts, who appears to be ice skating. An expert in early guerrilla warfare, Smuts commanded the Boer forces in the Second South African War (the Boer War). He later commanded the South African forces in World War I and held many South African government posts, including that of prime minister.

Returning to the northeast corner of Parliament Square, you'll see:

30. The Statue of Sir Winston Churchill, one of Britain's greatest statesmen, created by Ivor Roberts-Jones in 1973. Leaning on a stick, bulldog fashion, the World War II Prime Minister is looking across the street toward the Houses of Parliament.

WALKING TOUR 5

St. James's

Start: Green Park Underground Station.
Finish: Buckingham Palace.
Time: 2 hours.
Best Times: Monday through Saturday from 9:30am to 5pm.
Worst Times: Sundays, when shops are closed.

This small corner of London, nestled between Green Park and St. James's Park, has long been a favorite of the upper classes. The area called St. James's emerged around the Royal Palace of Henry VIII. In the belief that it is advantageous to be close to power, wealthy gentlemen erected splendid palaces and elegant homes for themselves near the palace. The 18th and 19th centuries were St. James's heyday—that's when most of the houses, shops, and clubs were built, many with riches gained from the British Empire.

The British class system is an outgrowth of the nation's past, though it may not be obvious to a visitor. The royal family remains a potent symbol of the importance the British still place on birth. In government, more than three quarters of the members of the House of Lords are hereditary peers; they inherit their seats as a birthright. Even today, many of England's nobility are wealthy simply because they own land that has been passed down for generations—land that was given to their ancestors by a king hundreds of years ago. Many of the buildings on this tour that are unremarkable for their architecture are spectacular for the culture they represent.

Leave Green Park Underground Station via the Piccadilly South Side exit. Turn right on Piccadilly and walk toward the Ritz Hotel. Just after the telephone boxes, turn right and go through the iron gates onto an unmarked pedestrian walkway called "Queen's Walk." On your right is:

1. Green Park, owned by the royal family, and so named because there are no flowerbeds. Although the reason for this lack is not precisely known, one popular story has it that King Charles II was walking here one day with his entourage when he announced that he planned to pick a flower and give it to the most beautiful lady present. When he gave it to a milkmaid from the local dairy, Queen Catherine became so enraged that she ordered all of the park's flowers removed. Over the years, Green Park has been the setting for duels, balloon ascents, and other events; to celebrate the peace of Aix-la-Chapelle in 1749, a spectacular fireworks display was arranged and for this occasion Handel composed his *Music for the Royal Fireworks.* Green Park is popular with picnickers, strollers, and patient British sun worshipers.

Continue down Queen's Walk and notice the still-functioning gas lamps that line this path. After the fifth lamp, turn left down the passageway that goes under several residential buildings (which, incidentally, are some of the most expensive apartments in London). After emerging on the other side—onto St. James's Place—turn right and walk 1 block to the grand:

2. Spencer House, 27 St. James's Place (tel. 071/409-0526), the ancestral home of Diana, Princess of Wales. The house, built for Earl John Spencer was begun in 1765 by John Vardy, a pupil of William Kent, but was completed by James Stuart after the shell had been constructed. The working gas lamps and torch extinguishers around the front door are typical of this earlier age. The building, which was restored by Jacob Rothschild in 1989 as a favor to Diana, is used now primarily for private functions; it is operated by the Spencer Trust. Although it is usually closed to the public, sightseers are admitted most Sundays from 10:45am to 4:45pm. A guided tour is scheduled every 15 minutes and admission is charged.

Next door to Spencer House is:

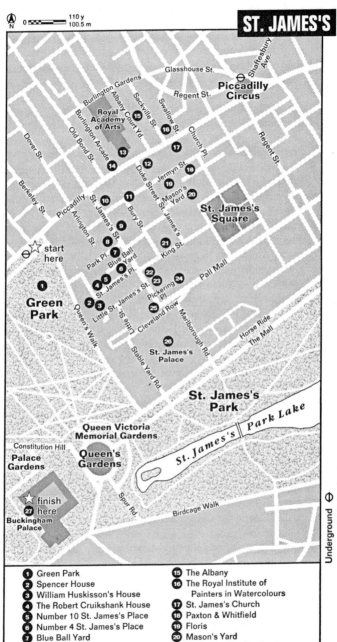

N
0 [scale] 110 y
100.5 m

Glasshouse St.

Regent St.

Piccadilly Circus

Shaftesbury Ave.

Burlington Gardens

Albany Court Yd.

Sackville St.

Swallow St.

Regent St.

Dover St.

Old Bond St.

Burlington Arcade

Royal Academy of Arts ⑮

⑯

Church Pl.

⑬

⑰

Berkeley St.

⑭

⑫

Jermyn St.

⑱

Piccadilly

Duke Street St. James's

⑲

Mason's Yard

⑳

St. James's Square

⑩ ⑪

Arlington St.

St. James's St.

Bury St.

㉑

⑨

Pall Mall

⑥ ⑦

King St.

☆ start here

Park Pl.

Blue Ball Yard

⑧

㉒

㉔

Queen's Walk

④ ⑤

St. James's Pl.

㉓

Pickering Pl.

① **Green Park**

② ③

Little St. James's St.

㉕

Cleveland Row

Marlborough Rd.

Horse Ride

The Mall

Stable Yard Rd.

㉖ **St. James's Palace**

St. James's Park

St. James's Park Lake

Queen Victoria Memorial Gardens

Constitution Hill

Palace Gardens

Queen's Gardens

☆ finish here

㉗ **Buckingham Palace**

Spur Rd.

Birdcage Walk

Underground ⊖

① Green Park	⑮ The Albany
② Spencer House	⑯ The Royal Institute of
③ William Huskisson's House	Painters in Watercolours
④ The Robert Cruikshank House	⑰ St. James's Church
⑤ Number 10 St. James's Place	⑱ Paxton & Whitfield
⑥ Number 4 St. James's Place	⑲ Floris
⑦ Blue Ball Yard	⑳ Mason's Yard
⑧ Brooks's Club	㉑ Christie's, The Auction Rooms
⑨ Boodle's Club	㉒ Lobb and Company
⑩ White's Club	㉓ Lock and Company
⑪ Jermyn Street	㉔ Pickering Place
⑫ Fortnum and Mason	㉕ Berry Bros. and Rudd Ltd.
⑬ The Royal Academy of Arts	㉖ St. James's Palace
⑭ The Burlington Arcade	㉗ Buckingham Palace

3. William Huskisson's House, 28 St. James's Place. A treasurer of the British navy in the early 19th century and archrival of the Duke of Wellington, Huskisson may best be remembered as the first person to be fatally injured by a steam-powered train; the accident occurred at the opening ceremony for the Liverpool–Manchester railway in 1830. It seems that Huskisson tended to be accident-prone.

Continue farther along St. James's Place where, on your left, you will see:

4. The Robert Cruikshank House, 11 St. James's Place, former home of one of London's most beloved satirical cartoonists. In the early 19th century, Cruikshank, together with his brother George, created the cartoon characters Tom and Jerry—two stylish and bawdy young men who were featured in a series of engravings called "Life in London" in 1820–1821. The cartoons, which were popular in both England and America, were the model for today's popular cat and mouse animated cartoons.

Next door you will see:

5. Number 10 St. James's Place—a building where the writer Oscar Wilde kept an apartment in the 1890s. It was here that Wilde met with several young men who testified against him at his homosexuality trial in 1895. (For more information on Wilde, see Stop 16 in the Chelsea walking tour.)

A few doors farther down the street is:

6. Number 4 St. James's Place, the house where the composer Frédéric Chopin (1810–1849) lived for one month in 1848. He was living here at the time he gave his last public performance—at Guildhall.

At the end of St. James's Place, turn left onto St. James's Street, walk a few yards, and turn left again into:

7. Blue Ball Yard, a delightful cobblestone courtyard that dates from 1741. Originally named for the Blue Ball Inn that once stood here, the yard is now the setting for some of London's most picturesque residences. You can see that these two-story buildings were once used as wine vaults and stables; look for the silhouetted images of horses' heads which hang above names such as "Farlap" and "Copenhagen."

Return to St. James's Street, turn left and cross Park Place. The next couple of blocks along St. James's Street are some of the swankiest in the world. Here are located some of London's most exclusive gentlemen's clubs. For centuries, these bastions of privilege have provided lodging, food, drink, and good company for the well-to-do. Women are not permitted on the premises of most of these clubs, and aspiring members may have to wait many years to be accepted. None of these clubs displays its name; they want to discourage attention from the general public, including sightseers (who are not permitted inside).

The ornate building on the far left corner of St. James's Street and Park Place is:

8. **Brooks's Club,** 60 St. James's Street. This building, which dates from 1778, was built for the Whig politicians who supported the American revolutionaries. The Whigs, who viewed the revolutionaries as fellow Englishmen, also wanted to escape the rule of King George III. One of the club's objectives was to collect money for "the widows, orphans, and aged parents of our beloved American fellow-subjects, who, faithful to the character of Englishmen, preferring death to slavery, were for that reason only inhumanly murdered by the king's troops at or near Lexington and Concord."

Notice the two lead water tanks on the left side of the club's front door. Look closely and you will see that the date "1776" appears on each, together with a depiction of St. George killing the dragon of tyranny.

With your back toward Brooks's, look across the street at the white building opposite. This is:

9. **Boodle's Club,** 28 St. James's Street. This building, which dates from 1775, is named after one of its earliest managers, Edward Boodle, a man who squandered his large inheritance and delighted in teaching young men to drink heavily! Not surprisingly, the club early on acquired a reputation for heavy gambling and good food. Past members have included the historian Edward Gibbon, who wrote *Decline and Fall of the Roman Empire,* the abolitionist William Wilberforce, the socialite George Bryan ("Beau") Brummell, and the Duke of Wellington. The room on the third floor, to the left of the venetian window, is the "undress dining room" for dining in informal clothes. Behind the venetian window is the club's main salon, which is 1½ stories high.

Continue 1 block up St. James's Street. The white building on your right, just past National Westminster Bank, is:

10. **White's Club,** 37–38 St. James's Street, the oldest and grandest of the St. James's gentlemen's clubs. This one was established on the site of White's Chocolate House, in a building that dates back to 1788. The club acquired an early reputation for around-the-clock gambling. The wagering sometimes went to extraordinary lengths, prompting one popular gentleman's magazine to note: "There is nothing, however trivial or ridiculous, which is not capable of producing a bet."

One 1750 report tells of a man who happened to collapse near the front door of this club. He was carried upstairs and immediately became the object of bets as to whether or not he was dead! One rainy day, it is said that Lord Arlington bet £3,000 on which of two drops of rain would reach the bottom of a window pane first. Bets were placed on births, deaths, marriages, public events, and politics—almost anything that came up in conversation or caused an argument.

Ironically, the club has a long conservative history and still claims many political Tories as members. Prince Charles is also affiliated with this club. When the Labour political leader Aneurin Bevan, who had once described all Tories as "lower than vermin," dined here in 1950, he was kicked in the bottom by a member (who was then forced to resign).

Walk two doors back on St. James's Street and turn left onto:

11. Jermyn Street, one of the most expensive shopping streets in the world. The small stores on both sides of this street are famous for their longstanding service to upper-class and royal clients. Most of the stores display Royal Warrants above their front doors—coats of arms that are given to those who sell goods to members of the Royal Family. The colorful shopfront of the royal shirtmakers—Turnbull and Asser (71–72 Jermyn Street)—on your right, is especially noteworthy, as is Taylor of Old Bond Street (74 Jermyn Street), a 19th-century-era beauty salon specializing in herbal remedies and aromatherapy.

Halfway down Jermyn Street, turn left onto Duke Street St. James's. The lime-colored building on your right is:

12. Fortnum and Mason, 181 Piccadilly (tel. 071/734-8040), the royal grocers. Enter the store at the Duke Street entrance.

Fortnum's, as it is affectionately called, was started by William Fortnum, a footman in Queen Anne's household. Since part of his job entailed replenishing the royal candelabras, Fortnum supplemented his income by selling the queen's partially used candles. When he retired in 1707, Fortnum opened this upscale grocery store together with his friend Hugh Mason. It was an immediate success, and by 1788 the shop had become world famous, shipping preserved foods and traditional specialties to English military, diplomatic, and other personnel overseas. Visitors to London's Great Exhibition of 1851—the first world's fair—came to Fortnum's to marvel at the exotic fruits and prepared foods and to buy picnic hampers—a tradition that survives to this day.

On June 16, 1886, a smartly dressed American man came to Fortnum's to meet with the head of grocery purchasing. Introducing himself as "a food merchant from Pittsburgh," the American gave Fortnum's grocer his first taste of horseradish, chili sauce, and tomato ketchup. Excited by these new tastes, the grocer enthusiastically said, "I think, Mr. Heinz, we will take them all." H. J. Heinz had arrived!

Exit Fortnum's main doors onto Piccadilly and look up at the glockenspiel clock above the front entrance. If you are lucky enough to be here on the hour, you will hear the clock chime the "Eton Boat Song," as the doors swing open to reveal little figures depicting Mr. Fortnum and Mr. Mason.

With your back to Fortnum's, cross Piccadilly. The large building to your left is:

13. The Royal Academy of Arts, Burlington House, Piccadilly (tel. 071/439-4996). Founded in 1768, The Royal Academy is the oldest society in England dedicated exclusively to the fine arts. Inside, you can see works by Reynolds, Turner, Gainsborough, Constable, and Stubbs. Michelangelo's *Madonna and Child with the Infant St. John* is also here; it's one of only four of the master's sculptures outside Italy. The Academy, which moved to this site in 1868, is also well known for its annual summer exhibition, where contemporary works are displayed and (often) sold. It's open Monday through Saturday from 10am to 6pm and there is an admission charge.

The Burlington House is the last of a half-dozen upper-class mansions that lined Piccadilly in the mid-17th century. Now one of the city's major commercial thoroughfares, Piccadilly was presumably named for a 17th-century dressmaker who invented a type of frilly collar called a "picadill."

Just to the left of the Royal Academy is:

14. The Burlington Arcade, one of London's first malls. There are no chain stores here, however. This elegant Regency shopping arcade has housed small, expensive boutiques since 1819. Tailcoated watchmen, called "beadles," continue to enforce the promenade's conservative code of behavior, making sure visitors don't run, yell, or whistle.

With the arcade on your left, walk down Piccadilly and take the first left into the courtyard of:

15. The Albany, a 1770 Georgian apartment building that is considered one of London's most prestigious addresses. Originally built for the First Viscount Melbourne, The Albany was sold in 1802 to a young developer named Alexander Copland, who commissioned the architect Henry Holland to convert the building into flats for single young men—actually, bachelor apartments. Many authors, playwrights, and poets have lived here, including Graham Greene, Aldous Huxley, J. B. Priestly, and Lord Byron. Pursuing her nine-month infatuation with Byron, Lady Caroline Lamb once managed to enter his Albany apartment disguised as a pageboy. Lady Caroline did not find Byron at home, but she wrote "Remember me" on the flyleaf of one of his books. Byron was so upset by this invasion of his privacy that he penned a poem that ended:

> *Remember thee! Aye doubt it not,*
> *Thy husband too shall think of thee,*
> *By neither shall thou be forgot,*
> *Thou false to him, thou fiend to me!*

Walk half a block down Piccadilly and look across the street at:

16. The Royal Institute of Painters in Watercolours, 195 Piccadilly, the former headquarters of the British School of Water Colour Painting. The school was established in 1831, and this building was constructed specifically for its use in 1882. Between every window you can see busts of those who founded the school, including that of J. M. W. Turner. When the school's lease on this building expired (in 1970), the institute moved here.

Cross Piccadilly at the traffic light and enter the courtyard of:

17. St. James's Church, 197 Piccadilly (tel. 071/734-4511), a postwar reconstruction of one of Sir Christopher Wren's loveliest churches. Consecrated in 1684 and known as "The Visitors Church," St. James's is indeed one of the most tourist-friendly chapels in the city.

To the right of the entrance is an old American Indian catalpa tree and a plaque that reads: "When tired or sad an American Indian will hug a tree to get in touch with earth's energy—why not you?" To the left of the entrance is a pulpit formerly used for outdoor noontime sermons. Today, the noise from cars on Piccadilly would probably make this impractical.

REFUELING STOP   The Wren at St. James's, 35 Jermyn Street (tel. 071/437-9419), is a delightful and inexpensive health food café and art gallery where you can enjoy such foods as carrot soup, fresh salads, a variety of sandwiches, and such pastas as vegetarian lasagna.

Enter St. James's Church and turn left into the main chapel. The interior of this church is exceptionally elegant; Corinthian columns support splendid barrel vaults decorated with ornate plasterwork. In 1684, the diarist John Evelyn expressed his view that "there was no altar anywhere in England, nor has there been any abroad more handsomely adorned."

The marble font at the rear left corner of the chapel is the church's greatest prize. Created by Grinling Gibbons, London's most famous Stuart-era sculptor, the intricate stem represents Adam and Eve standing on either side of the tree of life. The poet William Blake, among others, was baptized here.

The large organ at the back of the church was made in 1685 for James II's Chapel Royal in nearby Whitehall and given to St. James's in 1691. Its case was carved by Grinling Gibbons. Two British composers, John Blow and Henry Purcell, reportedly tried the organ soon after its installation. When the organ was being repaired in 1852, a miniature coffin containing a bird was discovered inside the instrument.

Near the fourth window on the left side of the church is a plaque honoring Sir Richard Croft, a 19th-century royal physician. His story is rather tragic. In 1817, Croft was caring for the pregnant Princess Charlotte—the only child of the Prince Regent. Because of pregnancy-related complications, Croft decided to bleed the princess and permit her very little food, hoping that this would cure her of a "morbid excess of animal spirits." After being in labor for 50 hours, Charlotte gave birth to a stillborn baby and the princess herself died a few hours later. Although the Prince Regent published a kindly tribute to Croft, the physician's reputation had been ruined. In February 1818, Croft was asked to care for another pregnant woman whose symptoms resembled those of Princess Charlotte. Before the birth, however, the doctor found a pistol hanging on the wall of the woman's house and shot himself.

Leave the church via the Jermyn Street exit, located directly opposite the door you entered. Turn right on Jermyn Street. Just ahead is:

18. **Paxton & Whitfield,** 93 Jermyn Street (tel. 071/930-0259), a store known not only for its cheeses, but also for its terrific meat and fruit pies.

A few doors down is:

19. **Floris,** 89 Jermyn Street (tel. 071/930-2885), the city's most exclusive perfumer. Notice the almost garishly large Royal

Warrant above the door. Floris has been making its wealthy clients smell nice since 1810; this old shop is something of a scent museum, and you may enjoy going in to see the delightful old display cases.

Continue on Jermyn Street for half a block and turn left, onto Duke Street St. James's. Walk 1 block and turn left, into:

20. **Mason's Yard,** a small square with some interesting associations. The lawyer's office on your left, at 6 Mason's Yard, was once the site of the Indica Art Gallery, a center for the 1960s avant garde movement. Shareholders in the gallery included the Beatles Paul McCartney and John Lennon. It was here that John Lennon and Yoko Ono first met.

Diagonally across the courtyard, to your left, you'll see **The Directors Lodge Club,** 13 Mason's Yard (tel. 071/930-2540). Now a hostess bar for men, this was formerly the site of a bar called "The Scotch at St. James," a 1960s favorite haunt of the Beatles, Rolling Stones, and others. It is claimed that Jimi Hendrix was "discovered" here.

Continue along Duke Street St. James's; after 1 block turn right onto King Street. Half a block ahead on your right is:

21. **Christie's, The Auction Rooms,** 8 King Street (tel. 071/839-9060), one of the world's best-known fine-art auctioneers. Established in 1766 by James Christie, a former navy midshipman, the establishment was moved to this location by the founder's son, James, Jr., in 1823.

Opposite the auction house is:

REFUELING STOP The **Golden Lion Pub,** 25 King Street (tel. 071/930-7227). A recent costly refurbishing has transformed this into one of the nicest pubs in the neighborhood. Fortunately, the quality of the food has not changed. Good pub lunches are served with Tetley, Burton, and other English ales; each month there is a "guest" beer.

Walk 1 block and turn left onto St. James's Street. Half a block down on your left is:

22. **Lobb and Company,** 9 St. James's Street (tel. 071/930-5849), shoe and bootmakers to the royals and the gentry. From left to right, the Royal Warrants above the door are from Queen Elizabeth, the Duke of Edinburgh, and the Prince of Wales. Inside, you can usually see a variety of wooden moldings of clients' feet used for custom-made shoes. Hidden in the shop's

vaults are centuries-old as well as contemporary moldings of famous royal feet, including those of Prince Charles, Princess Diana, Queen Elizabeth, and Prince Philip.

A few doors down is:

23. Lock and Company, 6 St. James's Street (tel. 071/930-5849), one of London's oldest haberdashers. Located at these premises since 1764, this hatmaker has covered some of the world's most important heads. Lord Nelson ordered a hat from Locke with a built-in eye patch; the Duke of Wellington bought from Lock the famous plumed hat that he wore at the Battle of Waterloo. It is said that the top hat was designed here in 1797. Its height caused such a furor that the first wearer was arrested and fined £50 for "going about in a manner calculated to frighten timid people." In 1850, William Coke, a gamekeeper, ordered from Lock a hard, domed hat for protection while chasing poachers. Produced by Thomas and William Bowler, Lock's chief suppliers, the hat became known worldwide as a "bowler." But around St. James's, the hat was called a "coke," after the man who had ordered it.

The narrow alleyway next door on your left is:

24. Pickering Place, the address of the Texas Legation from 1842 to 1845. Before Texas became a U.S. state, the Republic of Texas had its own diplomatic mission in Britain.

Enter the alleyway and walk to the delightfully quiet, enclosed courtyard. The buildings that surround you were constructed in the 1730s by William Pickering. Although you cannot see them, you are standing over a series of cellars where Louis Napoleon Bonaparte, later to become Napoleon III, may have plotted his return to France during his exile in the 1840s.

Return to St. James's Street; the building immediately to your left is:

25. Berry Bros. and Rudd Ltd., 3 St. James's Street (tel. 071/396-9600), wine and spirit merchants with Royal Warrants. If you drink Cutty Sark whiskey, you may recall the Berry Bros. name on every bottle. Notice the heavy 18th-century wooden shutters on the shop's front, which were heavily scratched by stones churned up by the wheels of passing carriages. Founded in 1696, Berry Bros. began as a grocery store; inside, you can see a huge set of scales that was brought in for weighing coffee. Uncommon in their time, the scales became popular with customers who often weighed themselves on them. For about 300 years, nearly 30,000 local people have weighed themselves here; their weights have been recorded in large ledgers. In addition to Lord Byron, Lord Nelson, and Lady Hamilton, we now have the recorded weight of King William IV (189 lbs., in boots); Queen Victoria's father, the Duke of Kent (232 lbs.); and others. The Fourth Baron Rivers weighed himself and had it written down almost 500 times. An entry for July 27, 1864, reads: "12 stone 4 lbs. at 1.30; 12 stone 5 lbs. at 2pm after two chops and a pint of sherry." [Note: 1 stone = 14 lbs.]

Walk half a block to the end of St. James's Street, which terminates at:

26. St. James's Palace, the official residence of the monarch. The palace, which dates from the reign of King Henry VIII, was the main residence of England's kings and queens for more than 300 years until Queen Victoria moved the royal residence to Buckingham Palace in 1837. Named for a convent that once stood on this site, St. James's Palace is today the headquarters of the Yeomen of the Guard and contains the Lord Chamberlain's office. Until recently, the ceremoniously garbed sentries who guard the front gate used to carry only swords. However, threats from the Irish Republican Army and others prompted the switch to bayonetted machine guns. If you see two sentries on guard, you'll know that the queen is in London; otherwise, you'll see only one sentry. By tradition, the stonefaced sentries are not supposed to talk. Feel free to take their pictures and try to make them laugh.

Turn right at the palace, walk to the end of Cleveland Row, and turn left onto Stable Yard Road. Pause at the security barrier to look at **Clarence House,** the home of Her Majesty Queen Elizabeth, the Queen Mother. Continue to the end of Stable Yard Road and you'll be on The Mall. Turn right and walk toward:

27. Buckingham Palace, the home of Queen Elizabeth II. Originally owned by the Duke of Buckingham, the house was later converted into a royal residence by George IV. John Nash, one of London's most productive architects, directed the renovation. The work was still not finished when Queen Victoria moved there in 1837, and successive modifications have enlarged the palace to almost 600 rooms. For tourists, the popularity of the palace itself is not due to its age or its architecture—it is neither old nor spectacular. But as home of one of the world's few remaining celebrated monarchs, the building is of symbolic interest. Although the public view is of the rather plain Neo-Georgian east front (added by Sir Aston Webb in 1913), the best view is said to be from the back, where the queen's famous garden parties are held.

The Changing of the Guard ceremony, performed by five rotating regiments of the Queen's Foot Guards, is held here daily in summer and on alternate days from August through March. (The ceremony is not held during bad weather, nor at the time of major state events.)

Beginning in 1993, it was planned to offer the public guided tours of Buckingham Palace during the months of August and September each year. Admission will be charged.

WALKING TOUR 6

Shakespeare's London

Start: Monument Underground Station.
Finish: Mansion House Underground Station.
Time: 2 hours.
Best Times: Daily 10am to 4:30pm.
Worst Times: After 5pm, when Southwark Cathedral and nearby museums close.

William Shakespeare was born 92 miles northwest of London, in Stratford-upon-Avon, on April 23, 1564. He came to London in his early 20s and immediately began working in theater.

Commercial theater, which was in its infancy in the 16th century, was banned from the City of London in 1576, in the expressed interests of hygiene and morality. Paradoxically, the ban stimulated the development of legitimate theaters and led to the construction of the first professionally managed, permanent stage—located outside the City limits, in Shoreditch. Called "The Theatre," Shakespeare performed on this stage before he became a partner with the owners, who rebuilt The Theatre on Bankside, Southwark, in 1599, and named it "The Globe."

Southwark (pronounced "sutherk"), located just across the River

Thames from the City of London, was already an entertainment quarter of bear gardens and brothels before the theaters arrived. The Globe was joined by several other playhouses, including The Swan and The Rose. Shakespeare staged many of his plays on Bankside, including *Hamlet, Macbeth, King Lear, A Midsummer Night's Dream, Twelfth Night, As You Like It,* and *Richard III.*

Southwark as an entertainment center was dealt a sudden death when the Puritans came to power and Cromwell became Lord Protector. The bankside theaters were shut; audiences caught at illegal performances were fined, imprisoned, and/or whipped; Southwark gradually declined. Today, it's an industrial and commercial center. This fascinating walk will take you through an area that is, unfortunately, overlooked by most tourists.

Exit Monument Underground Station at the Fish Street Hill exit and turn right onto Fish Street Hill. In the middle of the street, at the intersection of Monument Street, you'll see:

1. The Monument, a tall column built to commemorate the Great Fire of 1666. The fire is believed to have started just 100 yards to your left, in Pudding Lane. Shortly before 2am on September 2, 1666, an assistant to Thomas Farriner, the king's baker, was one of the first to smell smoke. Soon thereafter, London's Lord Mayor, Sir Thomas Bludworth, was awakened to observe the rapidly spreading fire. Believing it was inconsequential, Bludworth returned grumpily to his bed muttering, "A woman might piss it out!" Four days later, 90 percent of the city lay in smoke-blackened ruin; 13,200 houses, 87 churches, and 44 livery halls had been destroyed. Yet miraculously, only nine lives were lost.

Designed by Sir Christopher Wren to "preserve the memory of this dreadful visitation," The Monument was erected between 1671 and 1677. You can climb the 311 stairs of the 202-foot-high tower for a partial view of London's rooftops. There is an admission charge.

Continue past The Monument along Fish Street Hill to:

2. St. Magnus the Martyr, the church with the clock, at the bottom of the hill on your left. The striking steeple is one of Wren's finest. For centuries, the square in front of St. Magnus was an important center where locals congregated, official notices were read, and lawbreakers were punished. Situated near the head of the old London Bridge, the approach to the bridge used to pass in part through the porch of the church building. Miles Coverdale, who published the first English translation of the Bible (1535), was the Vicar of St. Magnus from 1563 to 1565.

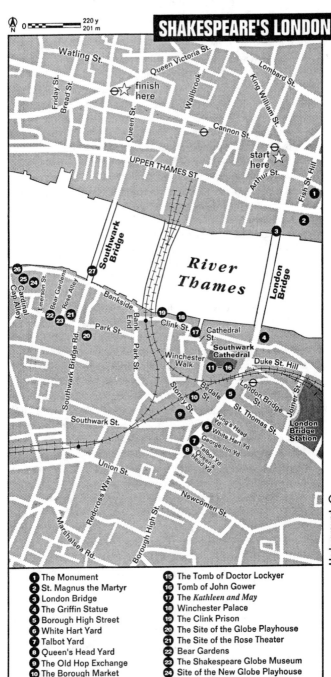

SHAKESPEARE'S LONGON

If the church is open, take a look inside—the interior was described by T.S. Eliot in *The Wasteland* as an "inexplicable splendour of Ionian white and gold."

Poke around the churchyard and you'll see some stones from the old London Bridge, as well as remains from a Roman-era wharf.

Exit the churchyard and turn left, onto Lower Thames Street. Walk beneath the overpass, then turn left, up the staircase, onto:

3. **London Bridge,** site of the first bridge to span the River Thames. The history of London Bridge is as old as the city itself—the Romans built the first bridge here around A.D. 75. It is not known how many wooden bridges may have replaced this original span, but when the bridge burned in 1014, the Norse poet Ottar Svarte was inspired to write: "London Bridge is broken down / Gold is won and bright renown . . ." a verse that would become the inspiration for the 17th-century nursery rhyme "London Bridge Is Falling Down."

Between 1176 and 1209, a stone bridge was built over the Thames with houses that lined both sides of the span. By Shakespeare's day, the bridge was home to a thriving community that surrounded a chapel dedicated to St. Thomas à Becket located at the bridge's midsection. London Bridge's narrow arches obstructed the river's tidal flow, allowing the Thames to freeze during the coldest winters. When it did, Londoners held frost fairs on the ice, with booths, sideshows, and barbecues. The houses came down in 1760 and the bridge itself in 1832. The five-arch stone bridge that replaced it did not restrict the Thames's tidal flow, and the river has not frozen over since. When the government decided to build a larger crossing in the 1960s, the old London Bridge was sold to the McCullough Oil Corporation, an American company that removed the old structure, brick by brick, to Lake Havasu City, Arizona.

Walk across London Bridge, pausing at the south end to look at:

4. **The Griffin Statue,** which marks the boundary between the City of London and the borough of Southwark.

Walk under the railway bridge that lies just ahead, and continue along:

5. **Borough High Street,** which in Shakespeare's day was a raucous road of debauchery, lined with taverns and inns. The 17th-century writer Thomas Dekker described the scene as one "continued ale house, with not a shop to be seen between." Notice that each street (or yard) you pass is named for an inn that once stood there. After King's Head Yard, turn left into:

6. White Hart Yard, the former site of White Hart Inn. A plaque on your right commemorates Shakespeare, who immortalized White Hart Inn in *Henry VI*, Part II, when Jack Cade declares: "Hath my sword therefore broke through London Gates, that you should leave me at the White Hart in Southwark."

In Chapter 10 of *The Pickwick Papers,* Dickens describes the White Hart Inn's "double tier of bedroom galleries, with old, clumsy balustrades . . . and a double row of bells to correspond, sheltered from the weather by a little sloping roof." The inn was demolished in 1889.

With your back to White Hart Yard, turn left onto Borough High Street, and left again, into George Inn Yard to:

REFUELING STOP   The George Inn, 77 Borough High Street (tel. 071/407-2056), the last surviving galleried coaching inn in London. The present building dates from 1676 and mimics the architectural style of London's earliest inns. An inn's front yard often doubled as a theater, in which strolling players would perform. Shakespeare's plays are still performed in this courtyard at noon on weekends during the summer. Charles Dickens, a frequent former patron, refers to The George Inn in *Little Dorrit*. Inside the bar you can see Dickens's life insurance policy; he gave it to the inn's landlord as security against his drinking bill!

Exit the George, turn left, and walk a few steps down Borough High Street to:

7. Talbot Yard, the pilgrims' gathering place in Geoffrey Chaucer's *Canterbury Tales.*

> *In Southwerk at the Tabard as I lay*
> *Redy to wenden on my pilgrymage*
> *To Caunterbury with ful devout corage,*
> *At night was come into that hostelrye*
> *Wel Nyne and twenty in a companye. . . .*
>   —"General Prologue"

The Tabard, which became the Talbot Inn, was demolished in 1873; all that remains now is an empty, strikingly dingy compound.

Exit Talbot Yard, turn left and continue down Borough High Street to:

8. Queen's Head Yard, yet another dilapidated court that once enclosed a bustling inn. A few slabs of granite, complete with scrape marks from wagon axles, are all that remains of the Queen's Head, a rowdy pub owned by the mother of John Harvard, who founded Harvard University. Born in Southwark in December 1607, Harvard inherited his mother's pub in 1637, sold it shortly thereafter, and emigrated to the Massachusetts Bay Colony. Harvard died the following year, leaving £600 for the establishment of a University College.

Backtrack up Borough High Street, bearing left at the fork across from White Hart Yard (where the soldier on a plinth commemorates the dead of the two World Wars). Cross Southwark Street to:

9. The Old Hop Exchange, a magnificent blue-and-white building where the price of hops was negotiated, and grain was bought and sold. Hops are an important ingredient in making beer, a beverage that was even more important in Shakespeare's day than it is today. Turn right on Southwark Street, then left (at The Southwark Tavern) onto Stoney Street. Take the first passageway on your right into:

10. The Borough Market, London's oldest fruit and vegetable market. Designed in 1851 by H. Rose, the market is still run by St. Saviour, the parish church.

Turn left at the junction in the center of the market, and walk down an even smaller passageway, keeping to the right. When you emerge at the end, turn left onto Cathedral Street to:

11. Southwark Cathedral, the principal church of the diocese of Southwark. Although a church has stood on this site since the 7th century, the present cathedral has its roots in the Augustinian Priory of St. Mary Overie, which was built here in 1206. When King Henry VIII "reformed" the monasteries, and confiscated church lands (1537–1539), this sanctuary became the parish church of St. Saviour at Southwark—the name by which Shakespeare would have known it. In 1905, a diocese of Southwark was created, and this church became Southwark Cathedral.

Although most of the building has been rebuilt and restored since the 13th century, fragments of the original priory can still be seen inside. The church's interior is particularly noteworthy for its beautiful choir, altar screen, and nave (the latter dates from 1894). Also significant are the gargoyles that are perched high above the cathedral's front porch. Visitors who want to take interior photographs must purchase (at modest cost) a permission slip from the cathedral shop.

Enter the cathedral, turn right, and walk down the aisle to:

12. The Shakespeare Memorial, a somewhat clumsy statue of an uncomfortably reclining bard. Erected in 1912, the memorial's most interesting feature is the frieze behind the statue depicting the borough of Southwark in Shakespeare's day. The Shakespeare Memorial Window, located above the statue, is a stained glass tribute to his plays; it is divided into three parts—for the comedies, histories, and tragedies.

Continue along the aisle, up the two steps, and turn left through the small gate to:

13. The Altar, packed with statues dating from the 19th century. The exquisite altar screen, which dates from about 1520, was a gift from Bishop Fox of Winchester. Look for a small stone on the floor that bears the name of Edmund Shakespeare, William's younger brother. Edmund died in December 1607, after contracting bubonic plague.

Leave the altar through the left gate, and bear right, toward:

14. The Effigy of a Knight. Carved in oak around 1275, this is one of the cathedral's earliest monuments. It was once believed that the statue's crossed legs symbolized the knight's participation in the Crusades. Now, however, scholars believe that the carving indicates that the knight wanted to participate in the Crusades, but did not.

Continue down the aisle (passing the Harvard Memorial Chapel—named for John Harvard, who was baptized in this church in 1607), walk down the three steps and turn right to:

15. The Tomb of Doctor Lockyer. The lengthy, and humorous epitaph on the reclining statue admonishes those who would mock Lockyer's great invention—a pill that guaranteed immortality.

A few steps ahead, on your right, you will see the colorful:

16. Tomb of John Gower, a poet and a friend of Geoffrey Chaucer. The statue of Gower shows his head resting on three of his most important works: *Vox Clamantis* (written in Latin), *Speculum Meditantis* (written in French), and *Confessio Amantis* (written in Middle English). The plot of *Confessio Amantis* is identical to that of Shakespeare's *Pericles, Prince of Tyre,* a fact that Shakespeare acknowledged by naming the chorus of his play "Gower."

Exit the cathedral and turn right onto Cathedral Street, which leads onto Clink Street, to:

17. The *Kathleen and May,* the last three-masted schooner to make regular cargo runs on the high seas. Just opposite the ship, walk straight, onto Clink Street, to the ruins of:

18. Winchester Palace, the home of the Bishops of Winchester for more than 500 years. Built in 1109, the palace often hosted meetings between church and state. Bishops of Winchester often doubled as officials in the king's court; thus, many important guests regularly stayed here. It is believed that King Henry VIII met his fifth wife, Catherine Howard, at this palace in 1540.

The last bishop to live here was Lancelot Andrews, who died in 1626. Shortly thereafter, during the English Civil War (1642–1652), the palace was turned into a prison for Royalist troops and was later rented out as apartments.

Redevelopment in this area during the 1970s exposed ancient remains of the palace's banqueting hall, which you can see today. You are looking at the west wall, which still has a magnificent rose window dating from 1330–1340. Beneath the window are three doors that once led to the pantry, kitchen, and buttery.

Walk around the bend of Clink Street (be careful of traffic) and go to the end of the block. The dark Victorian warehouses on either side of the street give this block a singularly sinister feel that has made Clink Street a popular location for filmmakers.

On the right wall, at the end of Clink Street, a wooden plaque commemorates:

19. The Clink Prison, which once stood near this site. Now synonymous with the word "prison," The Clink was a really nasty place for anyone in the 16th century. Henry Barrowe, John Greenwood, and John Perry were some of the jail's most prominent inmates. Persecuted for their religious beliefs, these men founded the independent, Southwark-based, church of Pilgrims (the group that emigrated to America in 1620).

Across the street is:

REFUELING STOP **The Anchor Tavern,** 34 Park Street (tel. 071/407-1577). This pleasant 18th-century riverside tavern stands on what is possibly the oldest pub site in London. The earliest record of a tavern at this site is from the 15th century. It tells of a pub known as the "Castell upon the Hoope," a name that literally means "The Castle on the Inn sign." Rebuilt and renamed in the 18th century, The Anchor has numerous hiding places and escape routes which, according to tradition, were used by prisoners from The Clink Prison next door.

The tavern, which is popular with local workers, serves standard pub lunches.

With your back to the river, walk along Bank End and take the first right onto Park Street. Two blocks ahead, on your left, is a plaque marking:

20. The Site of the Globe Playhouse, London's most famous theater. When the brothers Richard and Cuthbert Burbage inherited their father's theater in Shoreditch, in 1597, they decided to move it to this more lucrative riverbank location and form a partnership with some of the actors in their company, including William Shakespeare. The entire theater building was disassembled, shipped here, and it opened as "The Globe" in 1599. It would become the most important theater of the Elizabethan period. Shakespeare spent the rest of his career at The Globe, overseeing premieres and performances of 16 of his plays from *As You Like It* to *Pericles.*

The Globe was a circular structure, a wooden "O," with its center open to the sky. The stage was at the center of the circle, surrounded by seats on three sides and an orchestra gallery on the fourth. The most expensive seats were the covered galleries, located farthest from the stage.

Performances could take place only during daylight and when the weather was good. A flag was flown on the building's tall turret to let people in the City (just across the river) know that a performance would be held that day. A trumpeter would sound his horn across the water shortly before show time.

Walk under the Southwark Bridge on-ramp and pause at the corner of Rose Alley to see:

21. The Site of the Rose Theater. The Rose was the first theater established in Southwark's Bankside. Built in 1586–1587 by Philip Henslowe and his partner, it remained popular until it closed in 1603. Most of Christopher Marlowe's plays were presented here, along with works by other leading Elizabethan playwrights such as Robert Greene, Thomas Dekker, and Thomas Kyd.

Despite the fact that this theater was a competitor of The Globe, it seems that there was a relatively amicable relationship between the owners of both theaters. Historians generally agree that Shakespeare's *Titus Andronicus* and *Henry VI* both premiered at this rival playhouse.

Excavations of this site in 1989 provided archaeologists with much useful information about the structure of Elizabethan theaters. The developers of the office building that is now situated here have indicated that they might open a small museum on the premises to display artifacts that were unearthed during excavations.

Walk a few steps farther along Park Street and turn right onto:

22. Bear Gardens, an alley named for a bearbaiting ring that once stood here. The grotesque "sport" of bearbaiting pitted bears against other animals for the pleasure of the spectators. The matches were introduced to England by Italians, during the reign of King John. History tells us that Henry VIII came to watch, as did Queen Elizabeth I, who brought the French and Spanish ambassadors. The fights were not limited to bears, but included cocks, bulls, and dogs. In 1666, the diarist Samuel Pepys took his wife to a match where he noted that he saw "some good sport of the bulls tossing the dogs, one into the very boxes." In conclusion, Pepys confided that it was a "very rude and nasty pleasure." After visiting the arena in June 1670, the diarist John Evelyn wrote, "One of the bulls tossed a dog full into a lady's lap as she sat in one of the boxes at a considerable height from the arena. Two poor dogs were killed, and so all ended with the ape on horseback, and I was most heartily weary of the rude and dirty past time."

Just ahead on your right is:

23. The Shakespeare Globe Museum, 1 Bear Gardens (tel. 071/928-6342). Located in a converted 18th-century warehouse, on the site of a 16th-century bearbaiting ring and the 17th-century Hope Theatre, the museum displays a permanent collection of Shakespearean memorabilia and related artifacts. The primary exhibit traces the history of Elizabethan and Jacobean theater, which was centered in this area.

Continue to the end of Bear Gardens, where you can see an old stone stool set into the wall on the right. This was built for the ferrymen who operated boats that crossed the river from this point.

Turn left onto Bankside, and at the next corner pause at:

24. The Site of the New Globe Playhouse, a replica of the original, which is being built by the American actor Sam Wanamaker's International Globe Trust. As of this writing, the New Globe is scheduled to open on April 23, 1994 (Shakespeare's birthday).

Continue along Bankside to:

25. Cardinal's Wharf, 49–52 Bankside, a small collection of attractive white houses that are some of Southwark's oldest. The development is probably named after Cardinal Thomas Wolsey, who was Henry VIII's Lord Chancellor. In 1501 Catherine of Aragon, who later married Henry VIII, is said to have taken shelter here upon first arriving in London. And a plaque on Number 49 claims "Here lived Sir Christopher Wren during the building of St. Paul's Cathedral."

The coat of arms you see on Number 49 belongs to the Munthe family, the home's present owners. Numbers 50–52 Bankside were restored in 1712 as lodgings for the provost of Southwark Cathedral. The cathedral's coat of arms hangs outside.

Between the Cardinal's Wharf buildings is:

26. Cardinal Cap Alley, a small path squeezed between two buildings. The alley used to lead to Cardinal's Cap Inn, once the most popular meeting place for actors from the nearby Bankside theaters.

The area where you are now was also formerly known for its brothels. Some wits claim that this alley was actually named for a bordello—"The Cardinal's Cap"—which jokingly hung a red cardinal's cap on the hat rack in its entrance hall.

Backtrack along Bankside and climb up the stairs onto:

27. Southwark Bridge, a relatively modern span, completed in 1819. In Shakespeare's day, London Bridge was the only one across the Thames. Most theatergoers arrived by boat, transported from the north side of the river by ferrymen; at one time there were more than 40,000 ferrymen operating along the Thames between London Bridge and Windsor.

Walk across the bridge and turn left on Cannon Street to the Mansion House Underground Station.

WALKING TOUR 7

The East End

Start: Whitechapel Underground Station.
Finish: Liverpool Street Underground Station.
Time: 2 hours, moderately paced.
Best Times: Monday through Saturday from 9am to 5pm.
Worst Times: At night and Sunday (when many shops are closed).

The East End, an amorphous area hugging the City of London's eastern edge, encompasses two adjacent territories: Whitechapel and Spitalfields. From its beginning, the East End has been one of London's poorest areas. Traditionally, this location was undesirable because both the prevailing winds and the west-to-east flow of the River Thames carried diseases from the City and the hamlets to the west. Living on the "wrong" side of the City was dangerous indeed.

Spitalfields was once England's silk-weaving center, established in the 16th and 17th centuries by French and Flemish weavers. By the end of the 18th century about 17,000 looms were in operation, making weaving one of the largest businesses in the East End. Today little, if any, weaving is still done, but there are many reminders of the area's earlier history.

The East End has always been home to London's poorest

residents, many of them newly arrived immigrants from Ireland and the Continent, and in more recent years, from the Indian subcontinent and the Caribbean. At the turn of the century the East End was home to most of England's Jewish population, almost 90% by 1914, who lived in Spitalfields, Whitechapel, and St. George's to the east. They brought to the area a lively intellectual life. However, few Jews remain today.

The East End's most notorious connection is, of course, with Jack the Ripper, whose infamous series of still unsolved murders took place in Whitechapel in 1888.

Exit Whitechapel Underground Station and turn right onto Whitechapel Road. Just across the street is:

1. **The London Hospital,** a world-famous teaching hospital, founded in 1751. The hospital has the skeleton of the Elephant Man (not available for public viewing).

    Walk 2 blocks to the corner of Fulbourne Street, where you will see the site (now a pizza parlor) of the former:

2. **Jewish Socialist Club.** Once a hub of Europe's socialist movement, the club was a popular meeting place for top labor leaders. Socialism generally had a large following in poor Jewish neighborhoods, but especially in London's East End. The Hebrew Socialist Union was founded here in 1876, a Yiddish language anarchist newspaper *Arbeiter Fraint* ("The Workers' Friend") was established here in 1885, and the International Workers' Educational Club (colloquially known as the "Anarchist Club") was founded soon after. In May 1907, the Russian Social Democratic Labour Party Congress met in this building. The Congress delegates included Lenin, Stalin, Trotsky, Limnoff, and Gorky.

    Return to Whitechapel Road and continue for 3 blocks to:

3. **The Whitechapel Bell Foundry,** 34 Whitechapel Road (tel. 071/247-2544). One of the area's oldest establishments, the foundry has been casting bells in Whitechapel since 1583 (although it has been at its present location *only* since 1783). For more than 400 years this factory has been producing some of the most famous church bells in the world. The foundry's impressive credits include the bells of Westminster Abbey, Big Ben, and America's original Liberty Bell.

    Continue along Whitechapel Road, which becomes Whitechapel High Street. One block ahead on the left is a grassy area, formerly the site of:

4. **St. Mary's Church,** a 13th-century structure that was destroyed by bombs during World War II. It had been common procedure to limewash the exteriors of important buildings such

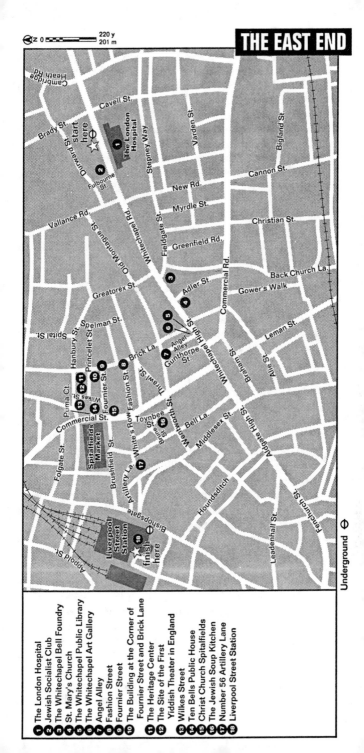

THE EAST END

220 y
201 m

Underground ⊕

1 The London Hospital
2 Jewish Socialist Club
3 The Whitechapel Bell Foundry
4 St. Mary's Church
5 The Whitechapel Public Library
6 The Whitechapel Art Gallery
7 Angel Alley
8 Fashion Street
9 Fournier Street
10 The Building at the Corner of Fournier Street and Brick Lane
11 The Heritage Center
12 The Site of the First Yiddish Theater in England
13 Wilkes Street
14 Ten Bells Public House
15 Christ Church Spitalfields
16 The Jewish Soup Kitchen
17 Number 56 Artillery Lane
18 Liverpool Street Station

as St. Mary's. Thus, it was this "Whitechapel" for which the entire area was named. Richard Brandon, the headman who beheaded Charles I (see Stop 11 in the Westminster & Whitehall walking tour) is buried in the churchyard.

Cross Whitechapel High Street and continue until you reach:

5. The Whitechapel Public Library, once the hub of London's Jewish intellectual community, a group that included the humanist Jacob Bronowsky, the mathematician Selig Brodetsky, the poet Isaac Rosenberg, and the novelist Israel Zangwill. These men, and others, met almost daily in the reference reading room where they exchanged ideas and debated intensely.

Next door is:

6. The Whitechapel Art Gallery, 80 Whitechapel High Street (tel. 071/377-0107). Built between 1897 and 1899, the gallery is housed in an unusual art nouveau–style building designed by C. H. Townsend. Founded by Canon Samuel Barnett, a local Jewish intellectual, the gallery originally displayed the works of the local Impressionist painter Mark Gertler. A lively lecture series attracted such luminaries as George Bernard Shaw. Today, frequent public exhibitions display some of the world's best modern art. Look for contemporary works that stretch the normal boundaries of art.

Just past the Art Gallery turn right into a narrow passageway called:

7. Angel Alley. Once an anarchists' meeting center, the alley is now the home of Freedom Press, a libertarian printer that produces some of the city's most left-leaning political literature.

Walk through Angel Alley, bear left up the steps to a small, nameless, cobblestone street. Turn right onto Gunthorpe Street, right on Wentworth Street, then left onto Brick Lane. Ahead, at the corner of Thrawl Street and off to your left, is a large housing development that stands on the site of **The Charlotte de Rothschild's Dwellings,** a low-income housing project built for poor Jews in 1886.

Continue 1 block along Brick Lane and turn left onto:

8. Fashion Street, which was at one time or another the home of several famous writers including the playwright Arnold Wesker and the Hollywood screenwriter Wolf Mankowitz. Israel Zangwill, the First Secretary of the World Zionist Federation, also lived here. Zangwill's first novel *Children of the Ghetto* was published in 1892, while he was working as a teacher at the nearby Jewish Free School. Zangwill's phonetic translations of East End speech won global praise but local scorn, which ultimately forced him to resign from the school.

Jack London was already a famous writer when he took up

residence here in 1902. London came to England to attend the opulent coronation of Edward VII. After the party, however, the writer was horrified to discover that so many Londoners lived in extreme poverty. London decided to "slum it" by living in the East End in order to learn first hand about the life of the city's poor. The writer's experiences are recorded in his book *The People of the Abyss,* an excellent ode to the East End at the turn of the century.

The three-story houses that line the right side of Fashion Street are typical of those where immigrants lived for generations. For decades, many of these buildings have also housed garment workshops; those working there now are the latest immigrants from Pakistan and Bangladesh.

Return to Brick Lane, turn left, and walk 1 block to:

9. Fournier Street, home of wool weaving in the 18th century, many of its factories still line both sides of this street. Notice the oversized attic windows, designed to maximize daylight on the workers' looms. A number of buildings on this street have been beautifully restored. The wooden shop front of J. Howard Gaze (37 Fournier Street) is particularly noteworthy; look at the painted ceiling through the upper-floor window.

If:

10. The Building at the Corner of Fournier Street and Brick Lane could talk, it could singlehandedly tell you the entire history of the East End. This massive structure's varied incarnations have reflected this immigrant area's changing demographics. Built in 1742 as a Huguenot chapel, the building was acquired 67 years later by the London Society, an organization established to convert Jews to Christianity. The Society offered £50 for each proselyte who agreed to resettle in a Christian district. However, in its final report of 1892, the Society admitted that, although it had spent thousands of pounds, it could claim only 16 bona fide converts. Ironically, the building's next occupants were Jews who transformed the premises into the Great Synagogue, Spitalfields. Abandoned in 1965, the structure was revitalized a few years later when it became a mosque, which it remains to this day, serving the area's Bangladeshi immigrants.

Just past the mosque, turn right, onto Princelet Street. At the end of Princelet Street, on your left (at the corner of Spelman Street), is:

 REFUELING STOP   The Alma, 41 Spelman Street (tel. 071/247-5604). This pub was established in 1854 by

Edward Tilney, a soldier who had just returned to London from the Crimean War. Built on the site of an old brewery, the pub's back garden still sports the original well head from which the water for brewing was drawn. Steve Kane, the tavern's ultra-friendly owner, is a former actor who loves to talk about his establishment's (and his own) eventful past. Tell him we sent you.

Backtrack up Princelet Street, cross over Brick Lane, and continue 5 doors on your right to:

11. The Heritage Center, Princelet Street, originally a string of weavers' homes with large attic windows. Look for the old weaver's symbol above the building's front door. In 1862 this center was transformed into a Liberal Jewish meeting place and house of worship called the Chevra Hidrath Chem ("Loyal United Friends Society"). In 1870, the Chevra bought the back garden of the house and built the United Friends Synagogue. This was the first intentionally built alternative synagogue in East London and the third-oldest Jewish temple in England. Although it no longer functions as a synagogue, the Bimah (the platform where services are conducted) still stands, the candelabra are still suspended from the ceiling, and the panels of the ladies' galleries are still covered with gilded inscriptions commemorating members of the congregation who contributed to its upkeep. In 1980 the building was bought by the Spitalfields Heritage Trust, which is now in the process of restoring it.

Continue to the end of Princelet Street and pause outside:

12. The site of the First Yiddish Theater in England, at the corner of Princelet Street and Wilkes Street. Founded in 1882, the Hebrew Amateur Society usually drew record crowds. Jacob Adler, one of the best-known actors of his time, often appeared here. On January 18, 1887, a false cry of "fire" during a performance caused a stampede that left 17 people crushed to death. Soon after this tragedy, Adler and his troupe emigrated to New York, where he helped found the American Yiddish theater, which substantially influenced the American theater as well as the Hollywood film industry.

Turn left onto:

13. Wilkes Street. Many of the houses on this street were built in the 1720s by Huguenot refugees who fled France after the revocation of the Edict of Nantes, in 1685. Many Huguenots were skillful silk weavers, and Spitalfields became famous for its quality silks. Wilkes Street was named after the political rabble-rouser John Wilkes, famous for his radical speeches during his 18th-century campaign for civil liberty. Many of the buildings on this block have been lovingly restored to their original Georgian splendor.

Turn right, onto Puma Court, then left onto Commercial Street. One block down, on the corner, you'll see:

14. **Ten Bells Public House,** formerly called "Jack the Ripper" because this pub is decorated with documents, papers, pictures, and photographs related to the infamous serial killer of 1888. Most of Jack the Ripper's murders occurred in and around these very streets, a fact that may be one of the East End's biggest tourist draws. The pub's design and furnishings are typical of the late 19th century.

Just south of Fournier Street is:

15. **Christ Church Spitalfields** (tel. 071/247-7202), a church built by Huguenot immigrants in 1720. A glance at the many 18th-century gravestones here reveals that a majority bear French names. The church's massive portico and barrel-vaulted arch are connected to the main body by an unusual, octagonal-spired tower. Services are held here only occasionally, as are classical concerts, but the church is usually open daily to sightseers. Call for a current list of events.

With the church to your left, continue down Commercial Street for 2 blocks; cross street to Brune Street, then turn immediately left onto Toynbee Street. Half a block down on your right is:

16. **The Jewish Soup Kitchen,** Toynbee Street. Opened in 1902 primarily to feed the area's Jewish poor, this kosher kitchen was busiest during the Great Depression, when it provided meals to more than 5,000 people each week.

Backtrack half a block and turn left onto Brune Street, then right onto Tenter Ground (named for the wooden frames over which woven cloth was stretched and dried). Turn left onto White's Row, which becomes Artillery Lane, a pleasant thoroughfare with bowed shop fronts. On your left you will see:

17. **Number 56 Artillery Lane,** a beautiful building dating from 1756 that is widely considered to be the finest Georgian storefront in London.

At the end of Artillery Lane, at Bishopsgate, is the back side of:

18. **Liverpool Street Station,** a major rail hub built in 1875 to accommodate the expanding population. Recently renovated, the station is the terminus for fast trains to the east and northeast London suburbs, as well as Britrail service to Cambridge, Norwich, and Harwich harbor.

WALKING TOUR 8

Clerkenwell

Start: Barbican Underground Station.
Finish: Farringdon Underground Station.
Time: 2 hours.
Best Times: Weekends, when less traffic permits a more pleasant stroll.
Worst Times: None.

Clerkenwell is a quirky little quarter, nestled in the center of London, between Bloomsbury and the City. Known as London's "hidden village," Clerkenwell's heyday came early—in the 17th century—when upper-class people built stately homes near the water well for which this area was named. Whether we realize it or not, however, most of us know the Clerkenwell of the 19th century because this was the stomping grounds of Charles Dickens, and many of the sights, smells, and sounds described in his novels he undoubtedly experienced in these very streets. Nineteenth-century Clerkenwell was highly industrialized, densely populated, and tragically poor. The area has since been revitalized, but many of the Georgian and Victorian buildings still remind us of this special area's colorful history.

Exit Barbican Station and turn left onto Aldersgate Street. Take the first left into Carthusian Street and walk 1 block on the right to:

1. Charterhouse Square, an unusual 14th-century cemetery. A number of catastrophes have befallen London over the years, but few have been as devastating as the bubonic plague—"Black Death"—which killed vast numbers of the city's population in 1348. Churchyards, the traditional burial grounds of the time, could not cope with the overwhelming number of deaths; consequently, deep pits (plague pits) for mass burials were dug in several open spaces throughout London. Have you guessed? Charterhouse Square is the site of one such pit, located just on the other side of this fence. The pit, which originally covered 13 de acres, was donated to the City of London in 1350 by Sir Walter Manny, a knight who sympathized with victims of the Black Death. Although the chronicler John Stow later claimed that 50,000 people were buried here, most historians do not believe that London's entire population at that time exceeded 35,000.

With the fence on your left, enter Charterhouse Square, walking past:

2. Florin Court, the art deco building on your right. This was the site of the offices of novelist Agatha Christie's detective Hercules Poirot.

Follow the fence around and step through the old wooden gates of:

3. The Charterhouse (tel. 071/253-9503), a retirement home for men who have served in the armed forces. The house was founded by Sir Walter de Manny in 1370 as a monastery for Carthusian monks. Built by Henry Yevele, King Edward III's master mason, the house enabled the monks to live in solitude six days a week. On Sunday, however, they came together in the refectory; this was the only time they were permitted to talk to one another—during a three-hour outdoor recess.

In 1535 the monastery's prior, John Houghton, invited Thomas Cromwell, then Henry VIII's vicar general, to a discussion on the king's supremacy as head of the English church. Cromwell responded by arranging for the monks to be imprisoned and tried for "treacherously machinating and desiring to deprive the King of his title as supreme head of the church." After his conviction, Houghton was hung, drawn, and quartered. As a warning to others, one of his arms was nailed onto the monastery's entrance gate.

The monastery surrendered to the king in 1537 and eventually it came into the possession of John Dudley, Duke of

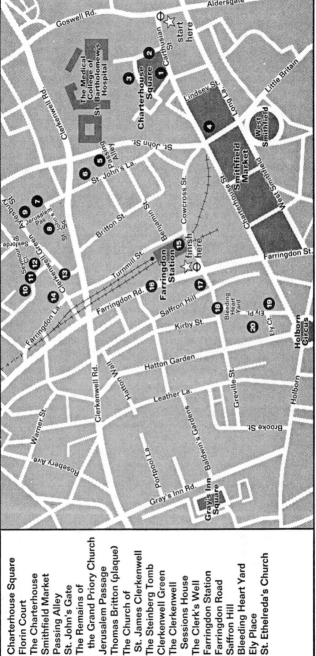

CLERKENWELL

1 Charterhouse Square
2 Florin Court
3 The Charterhouse
4 Smithfield Market
5 Passing Alley
6 St. John's Gate
7 The Remains of
   the Grand Priory Church
8 Jerusalem Passage
9 Thomas Britton (plaque)
10 The Church of
   St. James Clerkenwell
11 The Steinberg Tomb
12 Clerkenwell Green
13 The Clerkenwell
   Sessions House
14 The Clerk's Well
15 Farringdon Station
16 Farringdon Road
17 Saffron Hill
18 Bleeding Heart Yard
19 Ely Place
20 St. Ethelreda's Church

Underground ⊖

Northumberland. Dudley may have used The Charterhouse as a residence for his son, Guilford Dudley, and Guilford's wife Lady Jane Grey, who, in July 1553, was proclaimed queen upon the death of Edward VI; she was queen for nine days.

The Charterhouse was purchased in 1611 (for £13,000, a handsome sum at the time) by Thomas Sutton, who wanted the home to serve as a school for poor boys and men. Until 1892, the school successfully educated thousands of disadvantaged Londoners, including Baron Baden-Powell, who founded the Boy and Girl Scouts; William Makepeace Thackeray, the author; and John Wesley, who founded the Methodist Church.

Charterhouse is open to the public from April to July on Wednesday from 2:15 to 5:15pm.

Exit Charterhouse, turn right and continue through the iron gates to Charterhouse Street. On the right you will see:

REFUELING STOP   **The Fox and Anchor Public House,** 116 Charterhouse Street (tel. 071/253-4888). By law, London pubs are allowed to open from 11am to 11pm Monday through Saturday, and from noon to 3pm and 7 to 10:30pm on Sunday. But The Fox and Anchor is an exception. Known locally as an "early house," this tavern is specially licensed to serve alcohol between the hours of 6:30am and 9:30am, enabling it to accommodate the early-morning workers at nearby Smithfield Market, London's primary meat market.

If you are taking this tour early in the day, stop here for one of the pub's world-famous English breakfasts.

Across Charterhouse Street, on your left, is:

4. Smithfield Market, formerly the "smoothfield"—a grassy area just outside the city gates, where a weekly horse fair was held during the Middle Ages. In 1638 the City Corporation established a cattle market here. As the city expanded, encircling the market, residents complained about the general filth and drunken behavior of market workers. So, in 1855 the livestock market was moved to Islington.

Continue 1 block down Charterhouse Street and turn right, onto St. John Street. Cross to the left side of St. John Street and walk 2 blocks—past the White Bear Pub—turning left into:

5. Passing Alley, a small alleyway that served as a public toilet before modern sanitation measures were adopted. Before the advent of indoor plumbing, London sported a whole network of back alleys for pub-goers. Originally called "Pissing Alley," its name was changed only in the last century.

At the end of Passing Alley, turn right onto St. John's Lane and walk to:

6. St. John's Gate, once the main entrance to the 12th-century Priory of the Knights Hospitallers of St. John of Jerusalem, it is the only monastic gatehouse left in London. The priory no longer exists, but the gateway, which dates from 1504, has served a variety of functions.

During the reign of King Henry VIII (1509–1547), the gatehouse was used as office space for the king's administrators.

From 1731 to 1781 it was the headquarters of *Gentleman's Magazine,* a popular periodical whose contributors included Oliver Goldsmith and Samuel Johnson. Johnson was given a special room here in which to write; it is said that he literally locked himself away so that no one could get in and tempt him out or disturb him.

In subsequent years, the gatehouse was turned into the parish watch house; later, it became the Old Jerusalem Tavern. In 1874 the gatehouse became the property of The Most Venerable Order of the Hospital of St. John of Jerusalem, a Protestant order founded in 1831 to uphold the traditions of the medieval hospitallers. It was here that the St. John's Ambulance Brigade, one of the world's first, was founded in 1877.

Today, the gatehouse is still very much in use—as a museum and library.

Walk through the gate and continue straight ahead, across busy Clerkenwell Road. Proceed into St. John's Square. The iron gates on your right guard:

7. The Remains of the Grand Priory Church, the 12th-century church for which the gatehouse was the main entrance. All of the monastic foundations, which flourished in medieval times, were secularized by Henry VIII in 1540, leaving few traces behind. The remains of this church, located just north of the old city walls, are some of the best-preserved examples of those monasteries.

With your back to the church gates, bear right, into:

8. Jerusalem Passage, a small thoroughfare that was once the site of the priory's northern gate. It's an attractive street that flourished in the last century with small shops and boutiques. Most of the structures you see here today were erected on medieval foundations.

At the end of the short passage is a green wall plaque commemorating:

9. Thomas Britton (1644–1714), a local coal merchant and lover of music. Knowledgeable in chemistry, a respected collector of rare books, and a talented musician, Britton was widely known as "The Musical Coalman." A sort of Renaissance man, Britton established an informal music club that met above his rather dingy shop, formerly located on this site. The club attracted celebrated musicians of the day as well as members of the royal court.

Turn left on Aylesbury Street, then right, onto Sekforde Street, and left, onto Seymour Close, to:

10. The Church of St. James Clerkenwell, Clerkenwell Gardens. The original 1568 church was once a part of a Benedictine nunnery dedicated to St. Mary. Rebuilt in 1792 to include an elegant Wren-style steeple, the church became independent after the nunnery closed in 1849. Several monuments from the original church can be seen inside; if the building is open, it's worth a look.

The headstone located just to the right of the church's front steps marks:

11. The Steinberg Tomb, the grave of a murdered family. The Steinberg murders horrified the country when they occurred in 1834. Although the stone's inscription has worn away, you can still make out the name "Steinberg"—the surname of Ellen and her four young children who were stabbed to death on September 8th by their husband and father, John Nicholas Steinberg, before turning the knife on himself. Londoners were so distressed by the murders that they took up a collection to have Ellen and her children interred here at this church.

Since the murderer committed suicide, he could not be buried in a churchyard. Outraged citizens took Steinberg's coffin to a pauper's graveyard on nearby Ray Street. The burial took place at night; tipped from the coffin directly into the grave, the corpse was struck over the head with an iron mallet, and a stake was driven through its heart.

Exit the churchyard through the gates on the left and walk straight to:

REFUELING STOP   The Crown Tavern, 43 Clerkenwell Green (tel. 071/250-0757). Established in 1641 and rebuilt in 1815, The Crown gained fame in the 19th century because of its Apollo Concert Room, a live-music hall that was open every evening. The downstairs room of this bi-level pub still displays Victorian-era playbills. Today, the only entertainment is conversation among the patrons. A good selection of food and drink is always available.

The Crown is located on:

12. Clerkenwell Green, a busy street that is not "green" at all. In fact, for more than 300 years there has not been any grass here. Back in the 17th century, when Clerkenwell Green was surrounded by trees, the area was home to many knights and aldermen who built their mansions here. Clerkenwell's fall from exclusivity occurred in the 19th century when industry brought increased population and poverty. No longer a haven for the rich, the green became a meeting place for protesters.

With your back to The Crown Tavern, cross Clerkenwell Green to the Masonic Hall. This was once:

13. The Clerkenwell Sessions House, a former courthouse built in 1779 by the architect John Rogers. The stone sculptures adorning the front facade represent Justice and Mercy. By 1919, London's expanding criminal population had outgrown this building, and when the courts moved, the house was converted into offices. In 1979 the building was acquired by the Masonic Foundation and restored to its former glory.

Exit Clerkenwell Green onto Farringdon Lane, walk to:

14. The Clerk's Well, 16 Farringdon Lane, the water supply that gave the area its name. Peer through the windows of the building that now stands on this site, and you can see the remains of this well. St. Mary's Nunnery, located nearby, drew water from this well, which was originally known as the "Fons Clericorum," or clerk's well.

Return to Clerkenwell Road and cross it cautiously. Ahead, in the distance, you can see the lofty dome of St. Paul's Cathedral. Walk straight onto Turnmill Street and continue 4 blocks to:

REFUELING STOP The **Castle Public House,** 34 Cowcross Street (tel. 071/253-2892). Notice the symbol with the three balls fastened to the tavern's outside wall. This is the pawnbroker's emblem, and this pub is the only one in England licensed by Royal Decree to trade as a pawnbroker. One night, when the Prince Regent (later George IV) was gambling—and losing—nearby, he came in here and asked the landlord to advance him some money and to accept his watch as collateral. The publican duly obliged, and the very next day, a royal messenger redeemed the watch and, in the name of the prince, granted the pub a pawnbroker's license.

With your back to the pub, continue along Cowcross Street (named for its centuries-old association with nearby Smithfield Meat Market); on your right is:

15. **Farringdon Station,** part of London's first underground railway, built to carry traffic into central London. The station was opened in January 1863.

Just past the station is:

16. **Farringdon Road,** a major north-south thoroughfare constructed over the River Fleet. One of London's many underground rivers, the Fleet still flows approximately 28 feet beneath this road. The river had become polluted and something of a health hazard, and so it was paved over in the 18th century. Today it is an underground sewer.

Cross Farringdon Road and walk straight—to Greville Street. The next intersecting street is called:

17. **Saffron Hill,** named for the spice that was once sold here. In the 18th century, this area was part of the gardens of the Bishop of Ely. Saffron was popular in the days before refrigeration because of its ability to disguise the taste of rancid meat.

By the 19th century, Saffron Hill had become a notorious criminal rookery. Theft was so common it was said that you could have your handkerchief stolen at one end of the street and buy it back at the other! In his novel *Oliver Twist,* Charles Dickens referred to Saffron Hill, calling it "Field Court," the place where Fagin had his lair and where young children were trained in the art of pickpocketing.

Half a block down Greville Street on your left enter:

18. **Bleeding Heart Yard.** In 1576, early in her reign, Queen Elizabeth I decided to deed this land to her friend, Sir Christopher Hatton. The only problem was that she did not own the yard; it belonged to the Bishop of Ely. When the queen asked him to relinquish the land, he refused, prompting the queen to write: "Proud Prelate, remember what thou werst before we made thee. Comply, or by God we shall defrock thee." And so, the bishop complied.

Popular myth has it that Sir Christopher's wife, Lady Hatton, entered into a pact with the devil. One evening, in the midst of a party here, the devil appeared and took Lady Hatton, who was never heard from again. But, according to the legend:

". . . out in the courtyard, and just in that part where the pump stands—lay bleeding a large human heart."

The water pump is no longer here nor the heart, but the legend continues, encouraged by the yard's very name.

Exit Bleeding Heart Yard, continue along Greville Street, and turn left onto Hatton Garden. Turn left again, through the small doorway that leads to Ely Court. To your left is:

REFUELING STOP   Ye Olde Mitre Tavern, 1 Ely Court (tel. 071/405-4751). Built in 1546 for the servants of the Bishop of Ely, this beautiful Elizabethan pub was known to Dr. Samuel Johnson, Charles Dickens, and other famous local wordsmiths. Before you enter this ancient hostelry, look at the cherry tree that is now preserved behind glass by the front door. This tree used to be the boundary marker between the land the Bishop of Ely was allowed to keep and the land he was compelled to give Sir Christopher Hatton (in return for one red rose a year).

The Mitre Tavern offers a good selection of real ales and is justifiably famous for its toasted sandwiches.

Exit Ye Old Mitre, turn left onto Ely Court, and continue down the passageway, through the gates, to:

19. Ely Place, former site of the palace of the Bishops of Ely, until Queen Elizabeth I demanded that the land be given to Sir Christopher Hatton. The 19 charming houses that now stand here comprise the most perfectly preserved Georgian precinct in London. Until recently, Ely Place was controlled by the Council of Cambridgeshire, not London. As a consequence, the Metropolitan Police had no jurisdiction here and thus could not enter or arrest any suspect that walked through these gates. The property is protected by beadles, private guards with authority to eject anyone who causes a disturbance. To your right, at the end of the courtyard, you can see the beadle's hut with its white chimney.

The church hidden away on your left is:

20. St. Etheldreda's Church, Ely Place. Built at the end of the 13th century, the church was named for St. Etheldreda (St. Awdry), an abbess who died in A.D. 679 from a throat tumor that was said to have been inflicted upon her as punishment for her fondness for beaded necklaces. The type of devotional beads she wore—which were of cheap quality—came to be known as "St. Awdrys," which was shortened to "tawdrys"—a word that is still in use today.

Enter the church, which is best known for its ancient crypt and spectacular postwar stained glass. The arches of the crypt, which dates from 1251, architecturally combine Norman and Gothic styles.

Exit the church, turn right, and walk down Ely Place to Charterhouse Street. Turn left on Charterhouse Street, and left again on Farringdon Road to Farringdon Underground Station.

WALKING TOUR 9

Bloomsbury

Start: Holborn Underground Station.
Finish: The British Museum.
Time: 1½ hours.
Best Times: Monday through Saturday during daylight hours.
Worst Times: At night and on Sunday (when the pubs are closed).

Bloomsbury's convenient location, just north of Soho and west of the City, has been a significant factor in its development and charm. Bloomsbury's close proximity to businesses, shops, and theaters has long made this area a desirable place to live. Several large hotels and dozens of smaller bed-and-breakfasts testify to Bloomsbury's equal appeal to tourists.

Bloomsbury dates from the late 17th century; it was laid out around a series of squares that helped promote the area as London's newest social center. In the early 20th century, Bloomsbury gained fame for its large concentration of important writers and thinkers, including Clive and Vanessa Bell, E. M. Forster, Lytton Strachey, Bertrand Russell, John Maynard Keynes, and Leonard and Virginia

Woolf—who collectively became known as the "Bloomsbury Group."

The class system is still quite evident in Bloomsbury, where most of the land is still owned by a single person—the Earl of Bedford. The two largest occupants, however, are the British Museum and the University of London—institutions that keep this area alive with new faces and ideas. Bloomsbury has developed into a curious mix of private residences and public institutions—a well-balanced combination that seems to benefit everyone concerned. For the visitor, this means beautifully tended streets, historically significant buildings, interesting residents, and several major tourist attractions.

Leave Holborn Underground Station, cross High Holborn at the traffic light, and turn left. After 2 blocks, turn right into:

1. **Southampton Place,** an 18th-century street, named after the first Earl of Southampton. Several well-preserved Georgian houses, dating from the 1740s, line this block. On your left you will see:

2. **The House of John Henry, Cardinal Newman** (1801–1890), 16 Southampton Place. An eminent theologian, Newman became a leading member of the ill-fated Oxford movement, an attempt to return England's Protestant-based Anglican Church to its traditional heritage. Newman failed to convince England's relatively progressive clergy that his way was the right way, but his Oxfords, named for the university where the movement was based, went so far back to their religious roots that Newman became Roman Catholic!

Continue 1 block along Southampton Place until you reach the last building on the left next to Bloomsbury Square. This is:

3. **Colley Cibber's Birthplace** (24 Southampton Place). An acclaimed actor, poet, and producer, Cibber (1671–1757) is closely associated with Theatre Royal, Drury Lane, where he spent most of his working life. Cibber had a reputation for maintaining almost tyrannical control over his theater productions. One story claims that after a bit player fluffed his lines, Cibber shouted, "Fine him five shillings." When informed by an associate that the producer wasn't even paying the actor as much as five shillings, Cibber replied, "In that case, give him ten shillings, and fine him five!"

Turn left onto Vernon Place and cross the street at the traffic light. You are now on:

4. **Bloomsbury Square,** ringed by elegant Regency-style houses; this centrally located square is one of London's most famous greens. The first house on the left side of the square is:

0 ⊨⊨⊨⊨ 220 y
201 m

N

Euston Station

Eversholt St.
Chalton St.
Euston Rd.
Melton St.
Cromer St.
Gray's Inn Rd.

Gower Pl.
Gordon St.
Upper Woburn Pl.
Cartwright Gdns.
Judd St.
Regent Square

University College

Gower St.

Endsleigh Pl.
16 15
Tavistock Pl.
Marchmont St.
Coram's Fields

17
18
Gordon Square
19
Tavistock Square
14
Woburn Pl.

Bedford Way

Torrington Pl.
20
9
10
Guilford St.
Lamb's Conduit St.

21 22
8
Russell Square
Queen Square
11 13

Malet St.
7
Bedford Pl.
12

Tottenham Court Rd.
Store St.
23
Montague Pl.
British Museum
Southampton Row
Bloomsbury Square

25
27 finish here
Montague St.
Bloomsbury Sq.
Theobald's Rd.

Whitfield St.
Bedford Square
24
Bloomsbury St.
6 5 4
Vernon Pl.

26
Great Russell St.
3
2
1
start here

Rathbone Pl.
New Oxford St.
Bloomsbury Way
Row

Oxford St.
St. Giles Circus
High Holborn
Kingsway

Soho Square
St. Giles High St.
Endell St.
Drury La.

Dean St.
Charing Cross Rd.
Monmouth St.
Wardour St.
Old Compton St.

Cambridge Circus
Long Acre

Underground ⊖

---

1. Southampton Place
2. The House of John Henry Cardinal Newman
3. Colley Cibber's Birthplace
4. Bloomsbury Square
5. The Former Home of Isaac D'Israeli
6. Number 20 Bloomsbury Square
7. Russell Square
8. Number 24 Russell Square
9. Sir Samuel Romilly's House
10. Hotel Russell
11. Queen Square
12. The Church of St. George the Martyr
13. The Water Pump
14. The Tavistock Hotel
15. The Customs and Excise Building
16. The Jewish Museum
17. Gordon Square
18. Number 46 Gordon Square
19. Lytton Strachey's House
20. Dillon's Bookstore
21. Gower Street
22. The Bonham Carter House
23. The Dame Millicent Garrett Fawcett House
24. Bedford Square
25. The Thomas Wakley House
26. Number 42 Bedford Square
27. The British Museum

5. The Former Home of Isaac D'Israeli, author and father of the Victorian-era prime minister Benjamin Disraeli. Isaac was born in England to Sephardic Jews who had fled from persecution in Spain. Educated in Amsterdam, Isaac was both an intellectual and a respected writer. The older D'Israeli's literary works include *Curiosities of Literature* (1791), a volume of anecdotes and essays that went into 12 editions.

A few doors down, pause outside:

6. Number 20 Bloomsbury Square, the former home of Gertrude Stein (1874–1946) and her brother Leo. The Steins rented an apartment here in 1902, after Gertrude failed to get her medical degree at Johns Hopkins University in Baltimore. A voracious reader and writer, Gertrude enjoyed living near the British Museum's Reading Room, where she immersed herself in the works of the English novelist Anthony Trollope. But Stein complained of London's grim grayness; after spending a year on Bloomsbury Square, she left London for Paris, the city that would become her adopted home.

At the "top" end of Bloomsbury Square, cautiously cross Great Russell Street and continue straight onto Bedford Place. After 1 block, Bedford Place opens onto:

7. Russell Square, a grand old square that, because of its proximity to museums, hotels, and the Russell Square Underground Station, has become the de facto center of Bloomsbury. Constructed in 1800, the square is named after the Russell family, whose head is the Earl of Bedford, one of London's largest landowners. Because of its beauty and excellent location—close to both the City and the West End—Russell Square and the surrounding area has always been popular with lawyers, doctors, and other well-to-do professionals.

Turn left onto Russell Square and walk clockwise around the square to:

8. Number 24 Russell Square, where the poet T. S. Eliot worked as a book publisher with the firm Faber and Faber. In addition to being a successful writer, Eliot was also a prosperous businessman. In Eliot's time, as well as today, a rich writer was something of an anomaly. Eliot was generous to his less well-to-do friends. In his diary, fellow writer Roy Campbell (1902–1957) related that when he and Dylan Thomas were in need of money, they called on "his grace" (Eliot) and were rewarded lavishly.

Just a few doors ahead, along Russell Square, you will see:

9. Sir Samuel Romilly's House, 21 Russell Square. A lawyer and legal reformer, Romilly (1757–1818) is best remembered for his success in reducing the large number of offenses in England that were punishable by death. Romilly's own beliefs were clearly shaped by his Huguenot background. A brilliant tactician and convincing orator, Romilly's influence on English politics and policies should not be underestimated. Along with his friend and confidant, the abolitionist William Wilberforce, Romilly also played a significant role in stopping Britain's slave trade in the Caribbean and elsewhere.

Two blocks ahead, at the corner of Southampton Row, is the ornate:

10. **Hotel Russell,** perhaps the most beautiful building in Bloomsbury. Opened in 1900, the hotel's ornate facade is one of the finest examples of late Victorian Renaissance architecture in London and somewhat resembles the Houses of Parliament building and nearby St. Pancras train station. Prospective guests might want to know that, unfortunately, the interior (consisting of some 300 rooms) is not as elegant. Still, it's worth a look.

The hotel is on the site of the former Pankhurst house, once home to England's most famous suffragettes, Emmeline Pankhurst and her daughters Christabel and Sylvia. While living here, from 1888 to 1893, the Pankhurst sisters led the fight in England for women's right to vote and other forms of enfranchisement.

Continue around Russell Square and turn left after the hotel onto Guilford Street. Take your first right down a narrow passageway—Queen Anne's Walk—to enter:

11. **Queen Square,** a pretty plaza that was laid out in the early 18th century and named after Queen Anne. Once a fancy residential square, the green is now surrounded by hospitals and is a popular lunching spot for local workers.

One block ahead, on your right, you will see:

REFUELING STOP The Queen's Larder, 1 Queen Square (tel. 071/837-5627). This comfortable tavern serves good food and drink but deserves special mention for its unusual history. When King George III became mentally ill, he took up residence nearby, at the home of his attending physician, Dr. Willis. In order to help her husband, Queen Charlotte rented cellar space beneath this building to store some of her husband's favorite foods. This pub, The Queen's Larder—which means "pantry"—opened later in George III's reign.

Directly across the street from the pub is:

12. The Church of St. George the Martyr (1706), which is sometimes referred to as the "sweeps church." In the 18th and 19th centuries, poor boys—usually about 8 to 10 years of age—often worked to clean chimneys using their small bodies as brushes. Sympathizing with the plight of these impoverished youngsters, a local resident, Captain James South, established a charity at this church to help them.

Cross the street to the square's inside sidewalk and continue walking counterclockwise around the square. Pause at:

13. The Water Pump, located on the south side of the square. This iron pump, which dates from the early 1900s, commemorates the fact that Queen Square was once a water reservoir for the surrounding community. Times have changed, however, and the pump now carries a warning: "Unfit for drinking."

Continue around the square, step inside the gardens if you wish, and backtrack to the Hotel Russell. With the hotel on your right, walk 2 long blocks up Woburn Place to Tavistock Square. Turn left on Tavistock Square and stop outside:

14. The Tavistock Hotel, a large building that occupies the site of the former home of Leonard and Virginia Woolf. The Woolfs moved here in March 1929 and remained in Bloomsbury for 15 years. Virginia wrote in a large upstairs room that was illuminated by a skylight. The building's basement housed Hogarth Press, a publishing house that issued books by Woolf and T.S. Eliot, as well as English translations of the works of psychoanalyst Sigmund Freud. Virginia left this house just 19 months before she drowned herself in the River Ouse.

Walk counterclockwise around the square and stop at:

15. The Customs and Excise Building (on your right) where a blue wall plaque commemorates Charles Dickens, London's most famous Victorian author. From 1851 to 1860, Dickens lived and worked in a house that once stood here; this was a particularly prolific period in his life, during which he wrote the novels *Bleak House, A Tale of Two Cities, Little Dorritt, Hard Times,* and part of *Great Expectations.* Dickens's only surviving London home is located nearby (see Stop 29 in the Dickens's London walking tour.

Continue around the square to:

16. The Jewish Museum, Upper Woburn Place (tel. 071/388-4525), a small gallery that displays ritual objects and antiquities relating to Jewish life in England.

Continue straight for half a block and leave Tavistock Square via Endsleigh Place. After 1 block you'll enter:

17. Gordon Square, home of the Bloomsbury Group, London's most famous circle of writers, artists, and musicians in the early 20th century. Singing, dancing, reading, debating, and a fair amount of debauchery brought publicity to the group's regular soirées. But not everyone was impressed by the events and antics of the Bloomsbury Group. Gertrude Stein dismissed them contemptuously as "The Young Men's Christian Association— with Christ left out."

Turn left and pause outside:

18. Number 46 Gordon Square, the former home of John Maynard Keynes (1883–1946). One of the world's most eminent economists, Keynes played a leading role in the negotiations that led to the establishment of the International Monetary Fund, one of the world's most significant economic bodies. An enthusiastic host, Keynes turned his home into a meeting place for Bloomsbury's creative community. The gatherings were often attended by the writers Virginia Woolf and Lytton Strachey, as well as the ballerina Lydia Lopokova (who later married Keynes).

A few doors down you'll see:

19. Lytton Strachey's House, 51 Gordon Square. Strachey (1880–1932), a seminal writer and thinker, was an antiwar activist and conscientious objector during World War I. His well-regarded book *Eminent Victorians* is widely viewed as the first biographical novel—a new literary genre that mixed fact and fiction. When Strachey bought this house in 1919, he wrote to Virginia Woolf, "Very soon I foresee that the whole Square will become a sort of college, and *rencontres* in the garden I shudder to think of."

Turn right, around the square, and walk straight ahead on Torrington Place for 3 blocks. The Victorian Gothic building on your left, at the corner of Gower Street, is:

20. Dillon's Bookstore, 82 Gower Street (tel. 071/636-1577). Founded in 1937 by Una Dillon, a woman who had no previous bookselling experience, Dillon's has expanded to become the official bookshop of the University of London and one of the most famous booksellers in England. The eccentric poet Dame Edith Sitwell (1887–1964) was a regular patron of this shop and often gave impromptu readings to astonished customers. If it's not mobbed with students, the store is definitely worth a browse.

Turn left onto:

21. Gower Street, a pretty Bloomsbury thoroughfare that is popular with both students and tourists. About a dozen bed-and-breakfasts line the right side of the street, while most of the buildings on the left side are affiliated with the University of London.

One block down Gower Street, on your left, you'll see:

22. The Bonham Carter House, 52 Gower Street, a former surgeon's house and operating room. It was here, in December 1846, that the first general anesthetic was administered in England.

Three blocks ahead on your left is:

23. The Dame Millicent Garrett Fawcett House, 2 Gower Street. Fawcett (1847–1929) was one of England's most influential figures in the campaign for women's suffrage. Steadfastly opposed to militant tactics, Fawcett fought politically, rising to become the leader of the so-called constitutional wing of the suffrage movement.

Cross Gower Street into:

24. Bedford Square, Bloomsbury's last remaining wholly Georgian square. Laid out in 1775, the streets around the square were originally privately owned; access was limited to residents and to those who could justify their presence in the area. Many of the square's pretty doorframes are made of "Coade Stone," an artificial material that is known for its resistance to weather. When the Coade Artificial Stone Manufactory was closed in 1840, the secret of the stone's composition was lost, making these doorways the last of their kind in the world.

Walk counterclockwise around the square and pause outside:

25. The Thomas Wakley House, 35 Bedford Square. Wakley (1795–1862), a surgeon, founded *The Lancet,* England's most prestigious medical journal. He started the periodical in order to criticize medical malpractice and nepotism, an endeavor that involved him in numerous libel actions. While serving as coroner for the West Middlesex Hospital, Wakley often allowed the author Charles Dickens to attend his inquests, which provided Dickens with a lot of material for his novels.

As you continue walking around the square, take note of the house at:

26. Number 42 Bedford Square. This was once the home of the writer Sir Anthony Hope Hawkins (1863–1933), who is probably best known for his novel *The Prisoner of Zenda.*

Continue around Bedford Square, turn right onto Bloomsbury Street, then left onto Great Russell Street. The huge building on your left is:

27. The British Museum (tel. 071/636-1555). With its unmatched collection of important finds from Egypt, Greece, Rome, Cyprus, Asia, and the Middle East, the British Museum merits its own full-day walking tour. The Rosetta Stone, whose discovery in the 19th century enabled modern scholars to understand Egyptian hieroglyphics, is located at the entrance to the Egyptian sculpture gallery. A frieze from the Parthenon, known as the Elgin Marbles, is the most famous portion of the museum's extensive collection of Greek antiquities. They were named for Lord Elgin, who took them from Athens. The Greek government is suing to have these treasures returned, since they comprise an important part of Greece's cultural heritage. Also on display at the museum are 1,000-year-old Mesopotamian jewelry, Babylonian astronomical instruments, and Assyrian artifacts. Other fascinating exhibits include the contents of several Egyptian tombs, with their bandaged mummies. To the right of the museum's entrance, on the ground floor, are the **British Library Galleries.** Rotating thematic displays come from the library's collection of more than 8 million books. Included in the permanent exhibit is one of the two surviving copies of the Magna Charta (1215), Shakespeare's First Folio (1623), and a Gutenberg Bible (ca. 1453)—the first book printed with movable (hence, reusable) type. Autographed works by Bach, Mozart, and Handel are on display. You may be able to look into the British Library Reading Room, a hushed research room that was regularly used by Gandhi, Lenin, George Bernard Shaw, Virginia Woolf, and others. Karl Marx wrote *Das Kapital* here. The museum is open Monday through Saturday from 10am to 5pm, Sunday from 2:30 to 6pm.

Just opposite the museum you'll see:

FINAL REFUELING STOP   The Museum Tavern, 49 Great Russell Street (tel. 071/242-8987). Known as the "British Museum," until 1873, its location, across from the more famous British Museum, guarantees a touristy clientele. Still, the pub remains a popular refuge for local poets and scholars, making it a good place to end your tour.

Soho

Start: Leicester Square Underground.
Finish: Piccadilly Circus.
Time: 1½ hours, not counting café stops.
Best Times: Monday through Saturday from 9am to 10pm.
Worst Times: Sunday, when most of Soho's shops are closed.

Since the 17th century, Soho has been London's most cosmopolitan area. Although it is well known for its nightclubs, theaters, and restaurants, Soho is more than just nightlife. The district is a complex amalgam of the successive immigrant groups that have established restaurants and other businesses here over the last 300 years.

Strolling around Soho, it's not hard to find traces of the Victorian era adjacent to theaters from the 30s, beatnik cafés from the 50s, rock and roll hangouts from the 60s, pornography shops from the 70s, boutiques from the 80s, and dance clubs from last night. After all these years, Soho is still the best place in London to find a hidden restaurant or an all-night club.

London's entertainment district is also the center of the country's film industry. Within its borders can be found England's largest

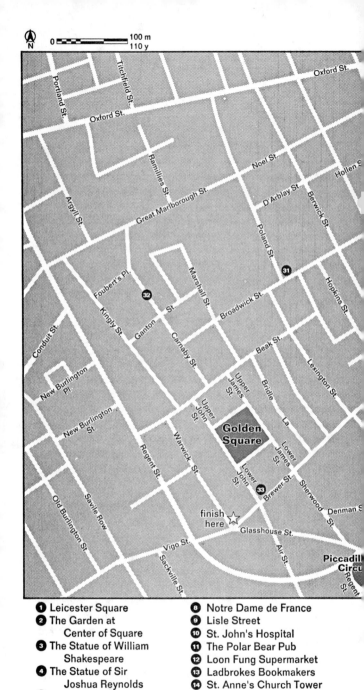

1 Leicester Square
2 The Garden at Center of Square
3 The Statue of William Shakespeare
4 The Statue of Sir Joshua Reynolds
5 The Statue of John Hunter
6 The Half-Price Ticket Booth
7 Leicester Place
8 Notre Dame de France
9 Lisle Street
10 St. John's Hospital
11 The Polar Bear Pub
12 Loon Fung Supermarket
13 Ladbrokes Bookmakers
14 St. Anne's Church Tower
15 Old Compton Street
16 Number 59 Old Compton Street
17 Meard Street

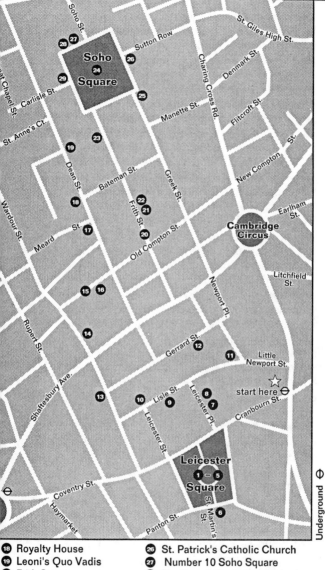

SOHO

Underground ⊖

18 Royalty House
19 Leoni's Quo Vadis
20 Frith Street
21 The Wolfgang Amadeus
   Mozart House
22 Ronnie Scott's Jazz Club
23 Hazlitt's Hotel
24 Soho Square
25 The House of
   St. Barnabus

26 St. Patrick's Catholic Church
27 Number 10 Soho Square
28 The French Protestant Church
29 Number 2 Soho Square
30 Number 17 St. Anne's Court
31 The Broadwick Street Pump
32 Carnaby Street
33 Number 71 Brewer Street

Chinatown, as well as a high concentration of cinemas, nightclubs, restaurants, and bookstores.

This walk will give you an excellent overview of all that Soho has to offer. After becoming acquainted with the area, return to Soho and explore those places that are of special interest to you.

Leave Leicester Square Underground Station via the Leicester Square exit and walk straight ahead to:

1. Leicester (pronounced "Lester") **Square,** Soho's most famous piazza. The site was known as Lammas Fields until the 1630s, when it was inherited by the Earl of Leicester, who built his mansion on what became the square's north side. The house became an alternative Royal Court in 1717, when the Prince of Wales (the future George II) took refuge here to escape the wrath of his tyrannical father, George I. Ironically, George II also became cruel to *his* son, Prince Frederick, who decided to move to Leicester House in 1742. Frederick later died, after being hit in the throat with a cricket ball on this square.

From the demolition of Leicester House in 1792 to the middle of the 19th century, the area of Leicester Square became rather dilapidated. There was a short-lived renaissance in 1851, when the geographer James Wyld erected a model of the Earth in a dome-shaped building that occupied the entire square.

A member of Parliament, Albert Grant, purchased this land in 1874 and commissioned James Knowles to design public gardens that would surround a memorial to Shakespeare and busts of four famous residents. Shortly thereafter, the London plane trees that now tower over the square were planted. A number of large legitimate theaters opened, including the Alhambra (1858), Empire (1884), and Hippodrome (1900). They dominated the area until the 1930s, at which time most of the theaters became cinemas or dance halls. In 1975 Leicester Square was permanently closed to traffic, and in 1990 the Westminster County Council had the square renovated.

Walk through the square's garden gates and enter:

2. The Garden at Center of Square. The statue on your right is of the satirical artist and illustrator William Hogarth, who lived at 30 Leicester Square from 1736 until his death in 1764. Trained as an engraver, Hogarth became popular for his biting portrayals of his contemporaries. While living on the square—then known as "Leicester Fields"—Hogarth produced his most famous works, including *Marriage à la Mode, The Rake's Progress,* and *Industry and Idleness.* His illustrations were often pirated, which led Hogarth to muster support for passage of the Copyright Law of 1735 (otherwise known as "Hogarth's Act").

Go to the center of the square and see:

3. **The Statue of William Shakespeare.** The scroll in the statue's hand reads "There is no darkness but ignorance." Just opposite is a statue of Charlie Chaplin; thus, the square is consecrated to theater and cinema.

Walk along the path that leads away from Shakespeare, noting the studs on the ground that indicate the distance to various countries. At the end of the path, you'll come to:

4. **The Statue of Sir Joshua Reynolds,** the celebrated 18th-century portrait painter and first president of the Royal Academy of Arts. Reynolds lived and painted at 28 Leicester Fields.

Walk to the center of the garden and, facing the back of Shakespeare's statue, take the path that forks to the right to:

5. **The Statue of John Hunter.** A contemporary of Reynolds, Hunter was a medical researcher who amassed a collection of more than 10,500 anatomical specimens, all of which were initially housed at his Leicester Square residence. A surgeon and anatomist, Hunter has been called the "father" of scientific surgery.

Just over the garden fence you can see:

6. **The Half-Price Ticket Booth,** where they sell discounted theater tickets for the day of performance only. The booth opens at noon for matinee shows, and from 2:30 to 6:30pm for evening performances. Payment must be made in cash (traveler's checks and credit cards are not accepted) and there is a small service charge.

Leave the garden and walk counterclockwise around the square, past the Moon Under Water Pub (once the site of the American painter John Singleton Copley's London home); turn right onto the pedestrian thoroughfare called:

7. **Leicester Place,** which was laid out and built in the 1790s by a banker named Thomas Wright. Half a block ahead on your right is:

8. **Notre Dame de France,** 5 Leicester Place, a church founded by a Marist priest in 1865. The facade has a statue of Mater Misericordia and the pillars portray eight scenes from the life of the Virgin Mary; they were created by students from the School of Fine Arts in Paris. The altar is constructed of Portland stone, and the frescoes in the Blessed Sacrament Chapel were painted in 1960 by Jean Cocteau, depicting the annunciation, Mary at the foot of the cross, and the assumption.

Continue to the end of Leicester Place and turn left onto:

9. Lisle Street, one of a half-dozen streets just north of Leicester Square that comprise London's Chinatown. A stroll here will reveal block after block lined with Chinese restaurants, grocers, and herbalists. Once concentrated in the Docklands area, east of the City, London's Chinese community—numbering some 2,000 people—began to migrate westward in the 1950s, seeking out new business opportunities. Chinese restaurants first opened in Soho after World War II to cater to British servicemen who had acquired a taste for this food overseas. At the time Soho was dominated by shabby brothels, seedy nightclubs, and run-down restaurants. Since short-term leases could be obtained for very modest sums, Chinese entrepreneurs began renting properties in this area and so Chinatown was born. Today, there are many inexpensive but good Chinese restaurants here, most specializing in traditional Cantonese cuisine.

Walk to the intersection of Leicester Street, where a plaque on the wall of Manzis Restaurant informs you that "Johanne Strauss 1st (1804–1849) Father of the Waltz dynasty lodged here (formerly Hotel du Commerce) on his first visit to England in April 1838."

On the opposite side of the street is:

10. St. John's Hospital (for diseases of the skin), 9 Lisle Street, which stands on the site of the former boyhood home of the actor Edmund Kean, who lived here with his uncle, Moses Kean. The boy was somewhat unruly, and he frequently disappeared into the labyrinth of Soho's byways. Eventually his uncle made him wear a brass collar with the inscription: "This boy belongs to number nine Lisle Street. Please bring him home . . . ."

Turn around and stroll the length of Lisle Street in the other direction, savoring the aromas from the various Chinese restaurants and grocery stores. At the corner of Newport Place is:

11. The Polar Bear Pub, 30 Lisle Street (tel. 071/437-3048). Formerly called the "White Bear," this tavern hosted some of The Rolling Stones' earliest rehearsals in 1962; their appearance was arranged by Brian Jones.

Turn left, onto Newport Place, then left again onto Gerrard Street—the bustling, colorful center of London's Chinatown. A few doors down, enter:

12. Loon Fung Supermarket, 42–44 Gerrard Street, a large Chinese market that sells unusual and exotic food.

The poet John Dryden (1631–1700) once lived in a house on this site, in an unhappy marriage. His wife once said that she would like to be a book so that he would pay more attention to her. Dryden replied, "Pray my dear . . . let it be an almanac, for then I shall change you every year!!" When she died, he composed an epitaph:

Here lies my wife, so let her lie
Now she's at rest and so am I.

Continue to the end of Gerrard Street, passing the two Chinese lions on your left; just beyond them (also on the left) notice the two Chinese-style telephone boxes. Where Gerrard Street intersects Wardour Street, you'll see:

REFUELING STOP   Wong Kei, 41–43 Wardour Street (tel. 071/437-8408). This is one of the least expensive restaurants in the area, and it features an extensive menu. At least a dozen popular dishes—including chicken with garlic sauce and beef with vegetables—cost less than a meal at McDonald's. As is true for most Chinese restaurants in London, if you want rice, it must be ordered separately. Tea is free.

Next to Wong Kei is:

13. **Ladbrokes Bookmakers,** an offtrack betting parlor and former home of the Flamingo Club, a popular folk music venue in the early 1960s. In the summer of 1964, singer/songwriter Paul Simon went on stage here for an impromptu performance. Later, Simon invited his friend, Art Garfunkel, to join him in a duet on the song "Sparrow"—this was the British debut of the team Simon and Garfunkel. Upstairs, in the same building, was a club called Whisky-a-Go-Go, a popular hangout for The Beatles and The Rolling Stones, and the site of David Bowie's 1984 video *Blue Jean.*

Turn right onto Wardour Street, cross Shaftesbury Avenue, and continue straight to the iron gates that guard:

14. **St. Anne's Church Tower.** An entire church once stood here. Dedicated to Queen Anne by her tutor, Henry Compton, the chapel was built by Sir Christopher Wren in 1678, and destroyed by bombs during World War II. Today, all that remains is this peculiar, beer-barrel-shaped church tower, designed by the architect Samuel Pepys Cockerell.

Walk through the gates and stand by the tower. Above the large tombstone on the wall to your right is a tablet commemorating Theodore, King of Corsica, "who died in this parish December 11, 1756." Forced from his kingdom, Theodore sought asylum in London but was soon imprisoned here for debt. The writer Horace Walpole composed the following epitaph for the king:

> The grave, great teacher to a level brings
> heroes and beggars, galley slaves and kings
> but Theodore this moral learn ere dead
> fate poured its lessons on his living head
> bestowed a Kingdom and denied him bread.

Exit the churchyard through the gates you entered, turn right on Wardour Street, and right again onto:

15. Old Compton Street, Soho's main shopping thoroughfare. It was named for Henry Compton, former Bishop of London.

On your right is:

16. Number 59 Old Compton Street, the former home of The 2 Is Coffee Bar. Popular in the 1950s, this café gained a reputation as one of London's earliest rock and roll hangouts. Ritchie Blackmore (from Deep Purple and Rainbow) played skiffle (jazz played on washboards, jugs or nonstandard instruments) here in 1960. A few years later, the adolescent Marc Bolan got a job behind the counter serving espresso here.

Cross Old Compton Street and take the first left onto Dean Street. Walk to the corner of:

17. Meard Street, a short street which was a private project by the carpenter John Meard—on the rowhouse wall, you can still see a plaque inscribed "Meards Street 1732."

Continue along Dean Street and pause outside:

18. Royalty House, a former theater where West End productions were staged for almost 100 years. Opened in May 1840 as Miss Kelly's Theater and Dramatic School, 10 years later it became the Royal Soho Theater. Soon thereafter the theater was converted to the New English Opera House, and then, from 1911 to 1938, it was the Royalty Theater until the Lord Chamberlain, who licenses theaters in England, withdrew its license. The present building dates from 1959.

Just across from Royalty House is:

🅟 **REFUELING STOP** The **Crown and Two Chairmen,** 31 Dean Street (tel. 071/437-8192). It is believed that Queen Anne came to Royalty House, across the street, to sit for a portrait being painted by Sir James Thornhill. Each day, the queen was transported to her sitting in a sedan chair (a kind of rickshaw), carried by two bearers. "The chairmen," as they were often called, retired to this pub for refreshment, and thus the tavern acquired its name.

Leaving the pub, continue a few doors along Dean Street and stop outside:

19. Leoni's Quo Vadis, 26–29 Dean Street (tel. 071/437-4809), a restaurant established by P. G. Leoni in 1926. Before it was a restaurant, however, this building was the former home of Karl Marx; he and his family lived in two small, upstairs rooms from 1851 to 1856. Marx and his family were subsisting on a small weekly sum given to them by their friend Friedrich Engels. Marx claimed that he rarely went out "because my clothes are in pawn." Three of his young children died here.

Retrace your steps back to the Crown and Two Chairmen. ("Sunset Strip," on your left, claims to have been the first strip club in the West End.) Turn left onto Bateman Street, then right onto:

20. Frith Street. Initially named for its builder, Richard Frith, this commercial street was eventually called "Thrift Street"; around the turn of the century its original name was restored.

A few steps down Frith Street, on your left, is the stage entrance of the Prince Edward Theatre. This building stands on the site of:

21. The Wolfgang Amadeus Mozart House, 20 Frith Street. Mozart was already a renowned prodigy when, at the age of eight, his family came here to stay for six months. A local celebrity, Mozart attracted attention whenever he and his sister took walks around the neighborhood. The young composer gave a recital of his own works in this house, performed on a miniature violin that was specially made just for him.

Continue along Frith Street to:

REFUELING STOP   **Bar Italia,** 22 Frith Street (tel. 071/437-4520). Soho's most authentic Italian café serves great espresso in a loud and busy atmosphere. Parma ham and cheese sandwiches are available at the bar; they can be eaten while standing or while seated at one of a handful of tables, which are usually occupied on weekends.

Look up at the building's attic where, in 1926, John Logie

Baird (1888–1946) presented England's first demonstration of television.

With Bar Italia on your right, retrace your steps along Frith Street and continue to:

22. Ronnie Scott's Jazz Club, 47 Frith Street (tel. 071/439-0747), the capital's best-known jazz room. Top international names regularly appear here, but be forewarned: this club is expensive.

One block ahead is:

23. Hazlitt's Hotel, 6 Frith Street, a formerly classy hotel, built in 1718. It was named for the essayist William Hazlitt (1778–1830), a Renaissance man who began as a painter but then turned to writing essays for popular critical magazines. Hazlitt died in this building, with the words: "Well, I've had a happy life."

Continue to the end of Frith Street (on your left you will pass the London headquarters of Twentieth Century Fox), which opens onto:

24. Soho Square, an attractive square that somehow seems out of place amid the theaters, clubs, and shops just a few steps away. Laid out during the reign of King Charles II, the square became home to the Duke of Monmouth, the king's illegitimate son. A gifted army officer, Monmouth made "Soho" the secret password at the Battle of Sedgemoore in 1685, where he was defeated in his attempt to oust Charles's successor, James II. Many of his co-conspirators were shot, but the duke himself was tried and later beheaded at the Tower of London.

The small black-and-white wooden structure at the center of the square is a toolhouse dating from the 1870s. Also in the square's gardens is a statue of Charles II, which dates from 1681.

Walking counterclockwise around the square, stop at the corner of Greek Street to see:

25. The House of St. Barnabus, 1 Greek Street, believed to have been the inspiration for Dr. Manette's house in Charles Dickens's novel *A Tale of Two Cities*. The house, which dates from the mid-18th century, is noted for its extraordinarily detailed interior, complete with carved wood, rococo plasterwork, and wrought-iron staircase. Now serving as a temporary shelter for homeless women, the house is open to the public on Wednesday from 2:30 to 4:30pm, and Thursday from 11am to 12:30pm.

Continue your circumnavigation of the square to:

26. St. Patrick's Catholic Church, which dates from the 19th century. Three hundred years ago, this was the site of the home of the Earl of Carlisle, a gentleman who befriended an eccentric inventor named Joseph Merlin. In the 1760s Merlin was working on what became his most notable invention—roller skates. One evening, during an elegant ball, the unorthodox Merlin demonstrated his skates by rolling at high speed through the mansion's salon, while playing the violin. Losing his balance, the inventor crashed through an ornate—and very expensive—mirror, thus ending both the demonstration and the ball.

Continue around the square to:

27. Number 10 Soho Square, a late-17th-century building that was once the home of Lady Mary Wortley Montague, a gifted intellectual and writer. She was a leader of society and fashion and the friend (or enemy) of most of the literary figures of her time. Her contemporary, Horace Walpole, once described her as "old, foul, tawdry, painted, plastered. . . . She wears a foul mop that does not cover her greasy black locks that hang loose, never combed, never curled. . . ." Lady Mary might have married the poet Alexander Pope, except that when he proposed to her, she laughed so long and loud that he immediately became one of her enemies.

Continue around the square to:

28. The French Protestant Church, erected in the 16th century "in grateful memory of H. M. King Edward VI who, by his charter of 1550, granted asylum to the Huguenots from France. . . ."

Continue to:

29. Number 2 Soho Square, home of MPL Industries—the former Beatle Paul McCartney's London office.

Exit Soho Square by turning right onto Carlisle Street. After 1 block, turn left onto Dean Street, and then right onto St. Anne's Court. One block down, at:

30. Number 17 St. Anne's Court, is a gray building that formerly housed the studio where The Beatles recorded several tracks of *The White Album,* and *Hey Jude.* The studio's grand piano was auctioned in 1989 for £30,000.

From St. Anne's Court, cross Wardour Street (home of many of London's important film companies) and Berwick Street (where a daily, lively produce market farther down on your left obscures from view the pornography shops that line this pedestrian thoroughfare), and walk straight onto Broadwick Street. Just ahead is:

31. The Broadwick Street Pump, a water pump that was

identified by Dr. John Snow as the source of the Soho cholera epidemic in 1854. Snow, a noted anesthetist who had studied cholera during a previous epidemic, theorized that polluted drinking water caused the disease. The doctor plotted on a map the addresses of more than 500 people who died in September 1854, and discovered that the Broad Street Public Water Pump (as it was then called) was at the geographic center of the epidemic. Snow's theory initially met with popular disbelief, but when the doctor had the handle of the pump removed, preventing it from being used, the outbreak soon ended.

Continue along Broadwick Street, past an elegant row of 18th-century houses, and turn left onto:

32. Carnaby Street, the "fashion" center of London in the 1960s. This pedestrian-only thoroughfare was laid out in the 1680s and named for Karnaby House, an apartment complex that originally housed a large number of Huguenot immigrants. The area slowly changed, and by the mid-19th century, Carnaby Street was the home of tradesmen who owned shops in the neighborhood. In 1957, retailers John Stephens, John Vince, and Andreas Spyropoulus opened Carnaby Street's first boutique—a men's store that soon attracted other small fashionable-clothing shops to the street. In the 1960s, Carnaby Street became synonymous with "flower power." A *Time* magazine article focused international attention on this street, and the *Oxford English Dictionary* defined "Carnaby Street" as "fashionable clothing for young people."

Today, the world of high fashion has moved elsewhere, but Carnaby Street still has a number of clothing shops that are worth looking at.

Walk to the end of Carnaby Street, turn left onto Beak Street, and then right onto Upper James Street. Continue through Golden Square to Lower John Street. At the corner of Brewer Street you'll see:

33. Number 71 Brewer Street, the former home of Chevalier De'eon. In 1762 De'eon arrived from France as an undercover agent for King Louis XV, who was planning to invade England. The invasion never materialized, but the Chevalier remained, befriending important Londoners and acquiring a reputation as one of the 18th century's most outrageous eccentrics. Part of his fascination arose from the fact that it was not clear whether the Chevalier was a man or a woman. His features were beautiful and his figure curvaceous, but De'eon drank heavily, smoked cigars, and was an accomplished equestrian and duelist. The Chevalier deliberately encouraged speculation by openly denying he was a man, although dressed as one. In gentlemen's clubs, bets were placed on his sex (seven to four that he was a man). Many of those bets were collected several years later, when the Chevalier began appearing in public dressed as a woman. By the time he died in 1816, at age 82, London accepted De'eon as a woman. When a postmortem examination revealed that he was, indeed, a man, the disclosure took the city by surprise.

Continue to the end of Lower John Street, walking under the two large arches that span the road. On the other side is Piccadilly Circus, where you can turn north on Shaftesbury Avenue to the theaters, south on Lower Regent Street to The Mall leading to Buckingham Palace, or east on Coventry Street to Leicester Square.

Chelsea

Start: Sloane Square Underground Station.
Finish: Sloane Square Underground Station.
Time: 2 hours.
Best Times: Wednesday through Saturday from 10am to noon, and again from 2pm to 4pm, when all the interiors included in this tour are open; Saturday on King's Road is particularly lively.
Worst Times: At night and on Sunday (when most shops on King's Road are closed).

Chelsea is an incredibly expensive residential area, but that wasn't always the case. Stretching along the Thames, south of Hyde Park and Kensington, Chelsea gained fame in the 19th century as London's Bohemia, a place for writers, artists, musicians, and thinkers. This beautiful "town within a city" was home to Thomas Carlyle, George Eliot, J. M. W. Turner, John Singer Sargent, Oscar Wilde, Henry James—the list of famous former residents seems endless.

But times change, and in the 20th century Chelsea was discovered

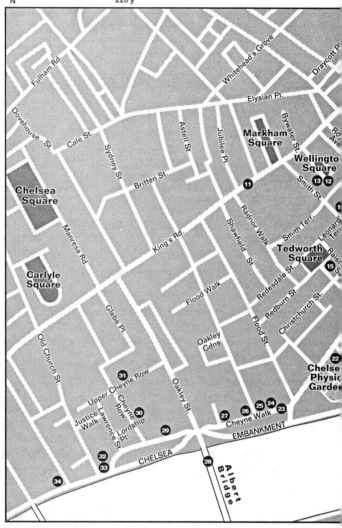

1. The Royal Court Theater
2. Sloane Gardens
3. Number 49 Sloane Gardens
4. The Old Burial Ground
5. Ranelagh Gardens
6. The Chelsea Royal Hospital
7. The Duke of York's Headquarters
8. Sir Laurence Olivier's House
9. Bram Stoker's House
10. Royal Avenue
11. King's Road
12. Wellington Square
13. Number 32 Wellington Square
14. Victorian-Era Mailbox
15. Mark Twain's House
16. Oscar Wilde's House
17. John Singer Sargent's House
18. The Studio of Augustus John
19. The Whitehouse
20. Paradise Walk
21. Clover Mews
22. The Chelsea Physic Garden
23. Cheyne Walk
24. George Eliot's House

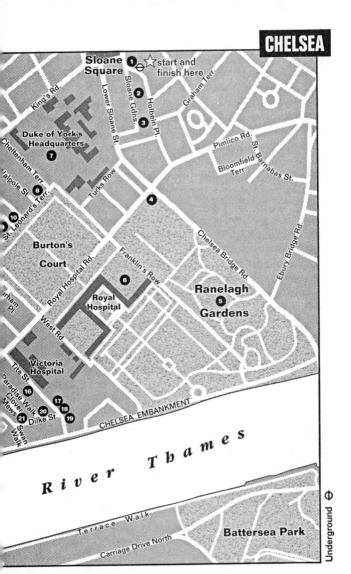

CHELSEA

by a new group of Londoners. Its location and beauty have turned the area into a favorite stomping ground of the monied classes. This tour will take you through one of the most beautiful urban neighborhoods in the world. Take a close look at Chelsea—you've probably never seen so many appealing homes that you'd like to own.

Exit Sloane Square Station, turn right, and walk a few steps to:

1. **The Royal Court Theatre,** Sloane Square (tel. 071/730-1745). Opened in 1888, the Royal Court quickly gained a top reputation by staging George Bernard Shaw's plays; many of them were rehearsed and performed here under his personal direction. After serving as a cinema in the 1930s and suffering bomb damage during World War II, the theater was rebuilt and became home to the English Stage Company—one of the city's most innovative theatrical groups. With the premiere of John Osborne's *Look Back in Anger* in 1956, the Royal Court has attracted many other leading dramatists to make their debuts at this theater, which is known for consistently high-quality productions.

Buy a ticket for the evening's performance, then retrace your steps past Sloane Square Station and continue straight ahead to:

2. **Sloane Gardens,** named for Sir Hans Sloane (1660–1753), who served as president of the Royal Society for 14 years. Sloane, who lived nearby, gained fame for his collection of more than 800 plant and animal specimens which he kept in his home. Upon his death, Sloane bequeathed 50,000 books and thousands of manuscripts to the British Museum—a windfall for their emerging collection.

The magnificent red brick houses at Sloane Gardens were built by the developer and parliamentarian William Willett who, incidentally, was also the chief campaigner for the establishment of Summer Time (Daylight Saving Time) in 1889.

3. **Number 49 Sloane Gardens** is the former home of the novelist and dramatist Egerton Castle (1858–1926), who lived here during the last years of his life.

At the end of Sloane Gardens, turn left onto Lower Sloane Street. Continue 2 blocks down to the traffic light and cross the road to:

4. **The Old Burial Ground,** the cemetery of the adjacent Chelsea Royal Hospital (see Stop 6, below). A soldier, Simon Box, was the first to be buried here, in 1692. Two of the more unusual stones are those of Robert Cumming and Joshua Cueman, which claim that upon their deaths—in the 18th century—the men

were aged 116 and 123, respectively. Another soldier William Hiseland's 1732 headstone says that he was in the army for 80 years and "when a hundred years old he took unto him a wife." It would appear that the Chelsea Royal Hospital had been extremely successful in preserving the lives of its patients! Only two women are interred here; both Christian David and Hanah Bell followed their lovers into battle in the Crimean War, each disguising herself as a male soldier. Their secrets were not discovered until they were wounded in action! For lack of additional burial space, the Old Burial Ground had to close in 1854; it is the final resting place of more than 10,000 former soldiers. Unfortunately, the cemetery is not open to the public, but you can see almost everything through the surrounding fence.

Turn right onto Royal Hospital Road; after 100 yards turn left, through two sets of gates, and on your left you'll see:

5. Ranelagh Gardens, one of 18th-century London's favorite outdoor areas. From 1742 to 1805, Ranelagh was the site of The Great Rotunda, an amusement park and meeting place for the city's upper classes. The 18th-century politician and man of letters Horace Walpole wrote, "Every night constantly I go to Ranelagh . . . my Lord Chesterfield is so fond of it that he says he has ordered all his letters to be directed thither." Today the Royal Hospital, which looms over the gardens, is the only remaining building in this park. With their gentle slope toward the Thames, the greens of Ranelagh are some of the prettiest in London and a pleasure to stroll. The gates you entered are this park's only entrance; they close daily from 1 to 2pm.

Leave the gardens and turn right. Retrace your steps a few yards and turn left into the central court of:

6. The Chelsea Royal Hospital. Although the competition is tough, we believe this building is one of the most attractive in London. Designed by Sir Christopher Wren (the architect of St. Paul's Cathedral), the hospital was founded in 1682 by King Charles II for men "broken by war and old age." Inspired by the Hôtel des Invalides in Paris, the Chelsea Royal Hospital still serves as a home for elderly, unmarried war veterans with no other source of income. Today, there are about 420 "Chelsea pensioners." Male veterans over 65 years of age receive food, shelter, and clothing plus a small weekly allowance, which they happily supplement by showing visitors around the buildings. The pensioners can easily be identified by their scarlet or blue uniforms and three-cornered hats, which they wear on special occasions.

The hospital's central court is flanked by two buildings. On one side is the chapel, featuring a relatively bright interior, which is typical of Wren churches. On the other side is The Great Hall, an awe-inspiring, wood-paneled dining room that would probably transform even the most mundane meal into an exquisite banquet. The painting on the left wall is of Charles II on horseback.

The Chelsea Royal Hospital is open to the public Monday through Saturday from 10am to noon and again from 2 to 4pm.

Back on Royal Hospital Road, cross the pedestrian walkway and continue straight ahead to Franklin's Row. With the private cricket grounds on your left, walk 1 block to:

7. The Duke of York's Headquarters, the large compound on your right, surrounded by an iron railing. Now used as a barracks for the Territorial Army—England's National Guard—the complex was originally built in 1801 as a school for war-orphaned children. The duke for whom this property was named was the second son of King George III and head of the English army. The Duke of York earned a reputation as a military reformer because he tried to stop the widespread buying and selling of army commissions. The number of officers who were unfit for their position had grown so large that the duke had to ask for the resignations of all colonels under the age of 20 and all captains under the age of 12! Ironically, it was later discovered that the duke's mistress was one of the people who were selling commissions, and the duke was forced to resign in disgrace. The Duke of York's Headquarters is not open to the public.

Turn left onto St. Leonard's Terrace and stop at:

8. Sir Laurence Olivier's House, 7 St. Leonard's Terrace, at the corner of Walpole Street. The great English actor lived here in the 1970s.

One block ahead, you'll see:

9. Bram Stoker's House, 18 St. Leonard's Terrace. Stoker (1847–1912), a prolific author, moved here in 1896, the year before his most famous book, *Dracula,* was published.

Walk back toward Olivier's former residence and turn left onto:

10. Royal Avenue, a romantically quiet and picturesque street lined with tall, red brick houses that were built in the early 19th century. The street was laid out in 1682 by Sir Christopher Wren; he intended for it to be part of a direct route from the Chelsea Royal Hospital to Kensington Palace. However, this short block was the only part of the project that had been completed by 1685, when King Charles II, the plan's sponsor, died. The rest of the route was never finished:

Walk to the end of Royal Avenue and turn left onto:

11. **King's Road,** Chelsea's primary commercial thoroughfare. Laid out in the 17th century, this busy shopping street originally was the king's road, a private street built exclusively for King Charles II, enabling him to travel from his London home to Hampton Court Palace. The only people allowed to use this road were the king and holders of a special copper pass with a crown on one side and the words "The King's Private Road" on the other. King's Road remained private until the 1830s. Now celebrated for its shops and boutiques, King's Road is one of London's best shopping streets. It is especially crowded on Saturday, when some of the city's trendiest young people turn the strip into a kind of informal fashion show.

Walk 2 blocks and turn left into:

12. **Wellington Square,** a delightfully picturesque horseshoe named for the Duke of Wellington. Built around 1830, the square has been home to several famous residents, including A. A. Milne (1882–1956), creator of Winnie the Pooh, who lived at Number 8 from 1904 to 1906, in what he later described as "two cheap and dirty rooms" at the top of the house. (Milne also lived nearby, on Mallord Street, for almost 30 years.) It was while he lived on Wellington Square that Milne wrote his first book *Lovers in London.*

Walk around the square to:

13. **Number 32 Wellington Square,** where the American novelist Thomas Wolfe (1900–1938) lived for a year, during which time he wrote *Look Homeward, Angel,* one of his best-known works.

Back on King's Road, walk 1 block and turn left onto Smith Street. On the next corner you'll see:

REFUELING STOP **The Phoenix Pub,** 23 Smith Street (tel. 071/730-7721), where you can avoid the tourists from King's Road and take a tipple with the locals. There are always special rotating "guest" beers, as well as the most popular brands. Food choices include sausages, sandwiches, and hot meat pies.

Continue 1 block down Smith Street where, at the corner of St. Leonard's Terrace, you will see a:

14. **Victorian-era mailbox.** Shaped like a pillar, the red box incorporates the Royal Badge (a lion and a unicorn) and the

initials "VR" (for Victoria Regina) above an extremely narrow mail slot.

Turn right and at Tedworth Square walk clockwise around the square to:

15. Mark Twain's House, 23 Tedworth Square. Author Mark Twain (Samuel Langhorne Clemens, 1835–1910) gained fame and fortune writing the American classics *The Adventures of Tom Sawyer* (1873) and *The Adventures of Huckleberry Finn* (1885). However, he lived extravagantly and invested poorly; thus, in 1891, the bankrupt Twain fled to Europe to escape his creditors. After his daughter, Susy, died in August 1896, Twain secluded himself in this house. The following year, *The New York Herald* newspaper set up a fund to collect money to repay Twain's debts, and so the writer was able to return to America.

At the bottom of Tedworth Square, turn left onto Tite Street, and walk 3 blocks to:

16. Oscar Wilde's House, 34 Tite Street. When the controversial Irish dramatist moved here in 1885, he was already a celebrity. The author of such works as *The Importance of Being Earnest* and *The Picture of Dorian Gray,* Wilde lived here for 10 years. It was here, in 1891, that Wilde was introduced to his lover, Lord Alfred Douglas, the son of the Marquess of Queensberry. Douglas's father disapproved of their relationship, and he often harassed the gay couple. Once, in 1895, the Marquess appeared at Wilde's doorstep with a whip, intending to lash the author for his "appalling" relationship.

There is another story about a man who tried to blackmail the writer with a letter that Wilde had written to Lord Alfred. When the would-be extortionist remarked, "A very curious construction can be put on this letter," Wilde had to agree. But the author added, ". . . art is rarely intelligible to the criminal classes." When the man realized that Wilde could not be blackmailed, he turned the letter over to the writer with the observation, "I am afraid you are leading a wonderfully wicked life."

Meanwhile, the Marquess of Queensberry continued to pursue Wilde. When he left a note at Wilde's club, The Athenaeum, addressed to "Oscar Wilde posing as a Sodomite," the author brought suit against the Marquess for libel. Wilde lost and became subject to prosecution as a homosexual, a criminal offense in England until 1967. The authorities gave him time to leave the country, but the defiant Wilde chose instead to sip champagne at the nearby Cadogan Hotel, where he was arrested. Upon conviction, Wilde was sentenced to two years of hard labor. When released, Wilde went into exile in Paris, where he died in poverty in 1900.

Continue 1 block farther down Tite Street to:

17. John Singer Sargent's House, 31 Tite Street. The American artist lived and worked in this house until his death on April 15, 1925.

Two doors down is:

18. The Studio of Augustus John, 33 Tite Street. One of the best-loved Welsh portraitists, John was a founding member of the De Stijl movement. He epitomized the English bohemian of the 1950s. The bearded, charismatic painter defied social convention in his dress, behavior, and way of life. An infamous womanizer, John attracted and mistreated numerous women.

Look at the light-brown brick building (with the lantern over the black door) about half a block down Tite Street, on your left. This was once the site of:

19. "The Whitehouse," a grand home built in the 1870s for the American painter James Abbott McNeill Whistler. While the house was still under construction, Whistler brought a slander suit against the art critic John Ruskin because of his review of Whistler's painting *Nocturne in Black and Gold: The Falling Rocket.* Ruskin wrote: "I never expected to hear a coxcomb ask 200 guineas for flinging a pot of paint in the public's face." Although Whistler won the case, he was awarded only one farthing (a quarter cent) in damages and was ordered to pay his own enormous legal costs. Temporarily bankrupt, the painter was forced to sell his beloved Whitehouse.

Turn right onto Dilke Street and right again onto:

20. Paradise Walk, a tranquil block lined with a pretty row of cottages trimmed with cute shuttered windows. The street wasn't always this bucolic, however; in fact, in the late 19th century, it was such a slum that Oscar Wilde erected a screen in his backyard so he wouldn't have to look at it.

Return to Dilke Street and take the next right onto:

21. Clover Mews, another pretty street that helps to make Chelsea one of the most desirable neighborhoods in London. The word "mews" comes from the French word *muer,* (meaning "to molt"). Originally a place where hawks were kept while molting, mews evolved to become buildings with stables on the ground floor and living quarters upstairs. Eventually "mews" referred to the small streets where such buildings were located.

Return to Dilke Street and take the next right onto Swan Walk. Look through the iron gate on your left at:

22. The Chelsea Physic Garden (tel. 071/352-5646), the second oldest physic garden in England (the one in Oxford is older). Originally established by the Apothecaries' Company in 1673 for cultivating medicinal plants, the garden has since expanded to include rare species from the New World. Behind its high walls is a rare collection of exotic plants, shrubs, and trees— many of them more than 100 years old. An unusual rock garden features stone from the Tower of London and basaltic lava from Iceland.

It is said that cotton seeds from this garden, sent to the Georgia colonist James Oglethorpe in 1732, began the great cotton industry of the American south.

The garden is open to the public from April through October only, on Wednesday and Sunday from 2 to 5pm. The resident English Gardening School holds lectures throughout the summer. Call for details.

Turn left around the gardens to Royal Hospital Road; after 2 blocks, bear right (across Flood Street) onto:

23. Cheyne Walk, one of the most celebrated streets in Chelsea. The houses on Cheyne (rhymes with "rainy") were built in 1720 and have been owned by famous people in the arts and entertainment field for more than a century.

A few steps ahead is:

24. George Eliot's House, 4 Cheyne Walk. For much of her life, the writer Eliot (Mary Ann Evans, 1819–1880) was enveloped in scandal for living with a married man, the literary critic George Henry Lewes. Often treated like a social pariah, Eliot found it extremely uncomfortable to appear in public with her lover. After Lewes died in 1878, Eliot became involved with John Cross, whom she later married. The couple moved to this address in 1880, but their time together was short, since Eliot died just a few months later—in December 1880. Upon his wife's death, Cross wrote in his diary ". . . and I am left alone in this new house we were meant to be so happy in."

Next door, at:

25. Number 6 Cheyne Walk, you can see an excellently preserved example of the block's original 1720s' architecture. Notice the two metal plaques above and to the left of the front door. These are insurance markers, indicating that the house was insured by two fire companies. Unlike modern-day practice, late 18th-century policies did not promise to repay damages. To have insurance meant that if your house caught fire, the company you paid would come to put it out; there were no public fire departments. The top plaque shows the clasped hands of the

"Amicable Contributors Company." The lower plaque, depicting a lion in a circle, was issued by the "British Fire Office."

One block ahead is:

26. **The Dante Gabriel Rossetti House,** 16 Cheyne Walk. The 19th-century painter and poet lived and worked in this handsome Tudor house from 1862 until his death in 1882. A member of the Pre-Raphaelite group, the artist moved here soon after the death of his wife, Elizabeth Siddal. When she was buried, the distraught Rossetti had a volume of his love poetry wrapped in her long hair and entombed with her. Seven years later, however, he had second thoughts about his romantic gesture, exhumed his manuscript, and published the poems.

Quite the eccentric, Rossetti turned his home into a sort of menagerie, filling it with a collection of exotic animals. In addition to a kangaroo and a raccoon, the artist kept a white bull, whose antics turned the garden into a wasteland. He also had a wombat that was much admired by his friend Lewis Carroll; it inspired Carroll to create the dormouse for *Alice in Wonderland.*

About 50 yards ahead on Cheyne Walk, turn right into:

27. **The tunnel** that runs between Numbers 23 and 24 Cheyne Walk. King Henry VIII's country house stood here until 1753 when it was demolished following the death of its last occupant, Sir Hans Sloane (see Stop 2, above). The cautionary sign at the entrance to the tunnel on your left reads: "All drivers of vehicles are directed to *walk* their horses while passing under this archway."

Return to Cheyne Walk and continue to the corner of Oakley Street. On your left you'll see:

28. **Albert Bridge,** one of the most picturesque spans in the world. Constructed at the height of the Victorian fascination with cast iron, it was designed in 1873 by R. M. Ordish.

Cross Oakley Street and continue along Cheyne Walk. One block ahead on your right is:

29. **Number 48 Cheyne Walk,** the former home of the Rolling Stone Mick Jagger, who lived here in the early 1970s. Band member Keith Richards still lives nearby.

At the corner of Cheyne Row and Cheyne Walk is:

REFUELING STOP   The Kings Head and Eight Bells, 50 Cheyne Walk (tel. 071/352-1820). Established around 1580, this intimate pub has long been a favorite of local writers and artists. The high concentration of luminaries who live in this area has always meant star clientele. The tavern's club-like atmosphere mirrors the exclusiveness of the surrounding neighborhood. In addition to a full line of ales and bitters, the pub boasts great food.

Turn right, onto Cheyne Row, and walk half a block to:

30. Thomas Carlyle's House, 24 Cheyne Row (tel. 071/352-7087)—the beautifully preserved former residence of one of Britain's most important essayists and historians. Carlyle lived here a long time—from 1834 until his death in 1881. The house, which dates from 1702, is now a museum administered by the National Trust. It is maintained much as it was in Carlyle's day, when the address was Number 5 Cheyne Row (notice that the "5" has been crossed out). There are still no electric lights on the upper floors.

While living here, Carlyle completed his epic *History of the French Revolution*. He lent the only manuscript of the first volume to John Stuart Mill, who, shortly thereafter, hurried to Carlyle's door to confess that his maid had "taken it for waste paper" and burned it. Carlyle had to rewrite the entire volume from memory, confessing at the end that he felt like a man who had "nearly killed himself accomplishing zero." A visit to this house is a *must*. It is open only from April to the end of October, Wednesday through Sunday and bank holiday Mondays from 11am to 5pm. There is an admission charge.

Walk half a block to the end of Cheyne Row and turn right, onto Upper Cheyne Row; a few yards down on your left is:

31. Number 22 Upper Cheyne Row, the former home of Leigh Hunt (1784–1859), an essayist and poet who lived here from 1833 to 1840. A contemporary and friend of the poets Byron, Keats, and Shelley, Hunt loved Chelsea and often wrote of this neighborhood:

"The end of the world. The air of the neighboring river so refreshing and the quiet of the 'no thoroughfare' so full of repose that although our fortunes were at their worst, and my health almost of a piece with them, I felt for some weeks as if I could sit still for ever, embalmed in silence."

Retrace your steps to the corner of Cheyne Row and continue straight ahead, where the road curves left into Lawrence Street. Walk 1 block down Lawrence Street, turn right onto Justice Walk, then left onto Old Church Street to:

32. Chelsea Old Church, the parish church of Sir Thomas More

(1478–1535). The building's beauty is diminished only by the heavy traffic outside and the fact that it and the surrounding area were heavily damaged by German bombs during World War II. Gracefully repaired, the church has a chapel that was designed in part by Hans Holbein, an urn that contains the remains of a man who owned most of Chelsea during the 1700s—Sir Hans Sloane—and a plaque commemorating the life of the American novelist Henry James, a long-time Chelsea resident who died nearby in 1916. The church's Lawrence Chapel is supposed to have been the scene of Henry VIII's secret marriage to Jane Seymour several days before their official marriage in 1536.

Outside the church, on the corner, is:

33. The Statue of Sir Thomas More, good friend and chancellor of King Henry VIII. When Henry broke with the Roman Catholic Church, More refused to accept the king as head of the Church of England—a stance for which he was subsequently beheaded on Tower Hill. More's story is depicted in the play and film *A Man for All Seasons.*

Cross Old Church Street; keeping the River Thames to your left, walk down the steps and through the sunken garden. At the end of the fence, turn right into:

34. Crosby Hall, an ornate reception hall that was once part of the home of Sir John Crosby, a wealthy wool merchant. The Hall was built originally in the early 1400s and owned successively by both King Richard III and Sir Thomas More. Its original, chapel-like brick and stone construction now has a modern wing of gray stone that was added in the 1950s. The hall has no identifying street number, possibly because it was transported here stone by stone in the early 1900s from Bishopsgate in the City of London, under the partial sponsorship of American-born Nancy Astor. Today the hall provides apartments and dining facilities for the British Federation of University Women. Part of the interior (which contains paintings by Holbein, a gracefully trussed roof, and some Jacobean furniture) is free and usually open to the public Monday through Saturday from 10am to noon and 2:15 to 5pm; Sunday from 2:15 to 5pm.

With your back to the river, walk up Old Church Street and turn right onto King's Road. From here you can either take a leisurely 1-mile stroll back to the Underground Station or catch bus number 11 or 22 for the return trip to Sloane Square.

WALKING TOUR 12

Hampstead

Start: Hampstead Underground Station.
Finish: Keats's House.
Time: 2 hours.
Best Times: Between 2 and 5pm, when Keats's House is likely to be open.
Worst Times: Sunday, when shops on Hampstead High Street are closed.

London's most famous suburb, Hampstead, gained fame as a 17th-and 18th-century spa resort. Situated on a ridge overlooking the City of London and the River Thames, Hampstead is centered around a heath (encompassing 785 acres of wild royal parkland) about 4 miles north of the center of London. In addition to high-rent homes and a bright shopping street, Hampstead's varied landscape includes formal parklands, woods, and ponds.

Hampstead's spas had fallen into disrepair by the middle of the 18th century, but the heath remained the traditional playground of the Londoner—the " 'Appy 'Ampstead" of cockney legend—which had been dedicated "to the use of the public forever" by special Act of Parliament in 1872.

"Leafy Hampstead," as it became known, has always attracted city dwellers who were eager to escape the grime and squalor of urban life. This suburb is most often associated with the landscape painter John Constable and the poet John Keats; regardless of famous residents and beautiful buildings, the walker will enjoy strolling around one of England's loveliest pastures.

Londoners are extremely proud of Hampstead Heath, and they love to go there for outings during nice weather. Even a short walk around this most handsome neighborhood will give you a deep appreciation for its unique qualities.

Exit Hampstead Underground Station and walk straight across Hampstead High Street to Heath Street. Continue straight, until you reach a pedestrian crossing. Cross the road and you will be at:

1. **Church Row,** often praised as one of most attractive streets in Hampstead. Most of the carefully preserved houses on this block, which date from the 18th century, seem to be unspoiled by time. Walk down the left side of Church Row, noticing that an old lamp bracket remains on the corner, guarding the memory of its bygone gas lamp.

A few doors down on your left is the former:

2. **Home of Lord Alfred Douglas,** 26 Church Row. He was the son of the Marquess of Queensberry but better known as Oscar Wilde's lover (for more information on Wilde, see Stop 16 in the Chelsea walking tour).

Continue straight ahead, toward St. John's Church, and walk through the wrought-iron church gates known as:

3. **The "Handel Gates."** They came from Cannon Park, Edgware, in 1747. It was there that George Frideric Handel served as composer for the Duke of Chandos.

Turn left immediately inside the church's gates and follow the rough, unpaved path that runs past the aged gravestones. At the end of this path turn right, onto the unmarked, paved path. Behind the fence to your left is:

4. **John and Maria Constable's Grave.** John Constable (1776–1837), one of England's greatest landscape painters, moved to Hampstead in 1819 so that his family "might enjoy fresher air than London could provide." Indeed, Hampstead provided Constable with much more than fresh air; it inspired him to create some of his best works. Over the next 15 years, Constable painted Hampstead's Heath, houses, trees, and clouds. By his own admission, Constable's happiest years were spent in Hampstead, of which he said, "Here, let me take my everlasting rest."

HAMPSTEAD

1 Church Row	**15** Number 2 Lower Terrace
2 Home of Lord Alfred Douglas	**16** Judges' Walk
3 The "Handel Gates"	**17** Whitestone Pond
4 John and Maria Constable's Grave	**18** Number 1 Elm Row
5 St. John's Church	**19** Home of Sir Henry Cole
6 Benham's Place	**20** Hampstead Square
7 St. Mary's Church	**21** Cannon Hall
8 The Watchhouse	**22** "Squires Mount Croft"
9 Abernethy House	**23** The Parish Lock Up
10 Number 6 Mount Vernon	**24** John Constable's House
11 Home of George Romney	**25** Number 1 Well Walk
12 Fenton House	**26** Burgh House
13 Admiral's House	**27** Downshire Hill
14 Grove Lodge	**28** Keats's House

Continue along the concrete path and turn right at the fork that goes through the trees to:

5. St. John's Church. The present building, which dates from 1745, rests on medieval foundations. When the structure was enlarged in the 19th century, the entire church was re-oriented, making it one of the few churches in the city with an altar that faces west rather than east (the direction of Jerusalem).

One hundred years ago, when the church's tower was confronting possible demolition, it was saved only through the efforts of such local artists as Anthony Trollope, William Morris, and Holman Hunt.

Enter the church's octagonal vestibule, which used to be the vestry. To your right are tablets listing all of the church's vicars, past and present. Directly ahead, on your left, is a bronze bas-relief of Henry Cort. According to Charles H. Morgan, the eminent American engineer who commissioned it, the bronze work honors the man "to whom the world is indebted for the arts of refining iron by paddling with mineral coal and of rolling metals in grooved rolls." Once you pass through the church's inner doors, you will see a charming gray-wood interior. Before you go down the central aisle, look to the left at the proud old font with the carved figure of John the Baptist on top. When facing the altar, you can see the church's old pulpit on your left. Above the radiator, to the right of the altar, is a bust of the poet John Keats, which was presented "to the English Nation" in 1894 by a group of his American admirers. Because Keats spent much of his life in Hampstead and wrote some of his finest works here, it was decided to place the statue in this church, rather than in Westminster Abbey.

Climb the stairs to the right of Keats's bust. The small cupboard on your right was built to hold the loaves of bread that used to be given to the parish's poor. Turning left onto the balcony, you can stand in front of the church's High Altar.

Exit St. John's and walk left down the pathway. Go through the gates and cautiously cross the busy road. Bear to your right and enter Holly Walk. At the end of the graveyard, look to your right at:

6. Benham's Place, a quaint street, lined with nine pretty cottages that date from 1813. These homes were built as part of a development undertaken by William Benham, a grocer and cheese-seller on Hampstead High Street.

A few yards down Holly Walk, on your right, is:

7. St. Mary's Church, a 1796 chapel built by and for refugees who fled their homeland during the French Revolution. St.

Mary's was one of the first Roman Catholic churches to open in London after the Reformation. General Charles de Gaulle worshipped here during World War II.

One block ahead, at the far corner of Holly Place, is:

8. The Watchhouse, 9 Holly Place, the 1830s' headquarters of Hampstead's first police force. Not everyone was pleased by the new constabulary, however. Many residents, including members of the local council, protested that police protection would place an undue burden on local taxpayers.

Step into Holly Berry Lane to savor its charm, then go back to Holly Place and turn right. At the end of Holly Place, go right, again, to Mount Vernon, and stop outside the first house on your right. This is:

9. Abernethy House, a former girls' school that became a lodging house in the late 19th century. Robert Louis Stevenson (1850–1894), who wrote *Treasure Island, Kidnapped,* and *Dr. Jekyll and Mr. Hyde,* stayed here several times. A booster of this charming suburb, Stevenson once remarked to a Scottish friend, "Hampstead is the most delightful place for air and scenery in London. I cannot understand how the air is so good, it does not explain itself to me. . . ."

Next door, at:

10. Number 6 Mount Vernon, you can see a metal plaque by the front door. This is an insurance marker—proof that the house is covered by a fire company. Unlike modern insurance, late 18th-century policies did not promise to repay any damage. Having insurance meant that if your house caught fire, the company you paid would come to put it out.

At the end of Mount Vernon is a blue plaque marking the home of the physiologist Sir Henry Dale. Walk along the pathway across from Dale's house and, at the fork, go around to the left. Walk to the end of the pathway and cautiously cross Holly Hill to Holly Mount. A short way down on the left side is:

REFUELING STOP   The **Holly Bush Pub,** 22 Holly Mount, Heath Street (tel. 071/435-2892). This tavern is closely associated with the 18th-century painter George Romney, who purchased several properties near here in 1796. When his health failed a few years later, Romney returned to his estranged wife in the Lake District; his stables were leased out and converted into this delightful, old-fashioned tavern.

The pub offers good food, served in several charming gaslamp-lit rooms. Burton and Tetley bitters are always on tap.

Leave the pub and walk to the end of Holly Mount, where you will be rewarded with a spectacular view over London.

Retrace your steps to the end of Holly Mount, passing the Holly Bush on your right. Stop outside the white building on your right, which is the former:

11. Home of George Romney, 4 Holly Mount. A relatively well-to-do artist who moved here in 1796, Romney (1734–1802) had deserted his wife several years earlier, saying "Art and marriage do not mix." The artist's success as a portrait painter ended in 1797 (only one year after he built this studio) due to physical and mental illness. According to Romney's biographer, a friend of the artist noted in 1799 that his "increasing weakness of body and mind afforded only a gloomy prospect for the remainder of his life." Romney left Hampstead that very year and returned to his wife in the Lake District, where he died a few years later.

Continue along Holly Mount, bear to your left across the green, and pause outside the magnificent wrought-iron and gold-leaf gates of:

12. Fenton House, Windmill Hill (tel. 071/435-3471), the oldest mansion in Hampstead, dating from 1693. Originally known as "Ostend House," it was owned by the silk merchant Joshua Gee, whose initials appear on the front gates. Gee had close American connections, and he is known to have traded with George Washington's father. The merchant imported pig-iron from Maryland and became a landholder in Pennsylvania.

Bequeathed to the National Trust in 1952, Fenton House now houses the Binning collection of furniture and porcelain (most of it dates from the 18th century) as well as the Benton Fletcher collection of early keyboard instruments (some of which you may play).

The house is open to the public only from April to October. There is an admission charge.

Continue past the house's gates and turn left down the gravel pathway called "Hampstead Grove." Turn left again onto Admiral's Walk, which ends at:

13. Admiral's House. Built around 1700, this house is notable for its roof, which, in 1791, was adapted to look like a ship's deck by Lieutenant Fountain North, who lived here from 1775 until his death in 1811. North even installed two cannons, which he would fire to celebrate royal birthdays and naval victories.

Sir George Gilbert Scott, the architect of Royal Albert Hall, lived here in the late 19th century.

Next door is:

14. Grove Lodge, former home of the novelist John Galsworthy (1867–1933). Best-known for his *Forsyte Saga,* Galsworthy won the 1932 Nobel Prize for literature. Too ill to receive his award in person, a delegation brought it to him here.

Continue to the end of Admiral's Walk and turn right onto Lower Terrace. Pause at:

15. Number 2 Lower Terrace, a small cottage that was rented by the artist John Constable during the summers of 1821 and 1822. Constable completed several oil paintings here, including one of Admiral's House and one of the shed in the back garden.

Turn left onto Upper Terrace and continue to the end, where you will see a small gravel pathway called:

16. Judges' Walk, a pleasant path with a view that was loved by Constable. Many of his paintings depict variations of this vista (and some include imaginary houses, a windmill, and even Windsor Castle!).

The Walk takes its name from the Great Plague of 1665, when city magistrates moved their court hearings outdoors to the edge of the heath in order to avoid possible exposure to infection from criminals and their accusers.

Do not walk on Judges' Walk. Instead, go through the small gap in the iron railing and continue along the rough pathway. Keep right until you reach Lower Terrace, where you should immediately turn left onto a very short gravel path. Cross West Heath Road and turn right to:

17. Whitestone Pond, a pretty lagoon named for a nearby white milestone that reads "4 miles from St. Giles pounds; 4½ miles from Holborn Barrs." When visiting his friend, Leigh Hunt, who lived close by, the poet Percy Bysshe Shelley (1792–1822) would come to this pond and sail paper boats with local children.

With your back to the pond, walk toward the traffic lights and ahead to Heath Street. Go down the left side of Heath Street, crossing Hampstead Square, and continue down the hill to the corner of Elm Row.

18. Number 1 Elm Row, former home of the author D. H. Lawrence for several months during 1923. Lawrence's experiences in Hampstead inspired his short story *The Last Laugh.*

Turn left onto Elm Row where, 1 block ahead on your left, is the former:

19. Home of Sir Henry Cole, 3 Elm Row. Cole, who founded Victoria and Albert Museum, lived here from 1879 to 1880.

Cole is also the person who originated the custom of sending Christmas cards.

Continue along Elm Row and turn left into:

20. **Hampstead Square,** which is actually not a square at all, but a park that was popular with street minstrels and actors who performed here in the 17th century. Later, Victorian tea gardens filled the square.

Bear right across the square (keeping the landmark Christ Church on your right) and continue straight to Cannon Place. Just ahead on the right is:

21. **Cannon Hall,** an 18th-century courthouse that was associated with the nearby lock up (see Stop 23, below). In the early 20th century, the hall was home to Sir Gerald du Maurier (1873–1934), father of the writer Daphne du Maurier and one of the last great turn-of-the-century actor/managers. Du Maurier made his mark with inspired interpretations of J. M. Barrie's plays and as the original Captain Hook in *Peter Pan.*

Around the corner are the three old cannons for which the hall and place are probably named. At one time the cannons served as hitching posts.

With your back to Cannon Hall, cross Cannon Lane and walk to Squires Mount. The row of cottages a little way down on your right is called:

22. **"Squires Mount Croft."** Built in 1704, these are the oldest terrace homes in Hampstead.

Retrace your steps to Cannon Hall and, with the wall on your right, continue down Cannon Place to:

23. **The Parish Lock Up,** 11 Cannon Place, an 18th-century jailhouse. Before the government assumed responsibility for law enforcement, this was a function of local churches. This Parish Lock Up was built into the garden wall of Cannon Hall in the 1730s. The single, dark cell was a holding pen where prisoners were kept until other arrangements could be made. Soon after the local police force was established in 1829, the lock up was moved to the Watch House in Holly Walk. This is one of the few parish lock ups remaining in London.

At the end of Cannon Lane, cross Well Road and take the small pathway directly opposite to Well Walk. Turn right at the fountain. A few doors down on your left is:

24. **John Constable's House,** 40 Well Walk. Constable lived here from 1827 until his death 10 years later. The artist's wife, Maria, developed pulmonary consumption soon after their seventh child was born, at the beginning of 1828. A friend who visited the house shortly before Maria's death recalled how

Constable appeared to be his usual self in his wife's presence. But later on, when the artist took him into another room, Constable burst into tears without speaking. Despite his sorrow, Constable maintained a caustic wit. Once he told the Hampstead dairyman, "In the future we shall feel obliged if you will send us the milk and the water in separate cans."

Continue along Well Walk to the building next to The Wells Tavern. This is:

25. Number 1 Well Walk, site of a former home of John Keats, the poet. Keats moved here with his brother, Tom, in 1817, the same year that his first volume of poems was published. The book's sales proved disappointing, however, and the publishers expressed regret over their involvement with Keats and his manuscript.

Tom Keats was seriously ill while he lived here, and he relied on his brother to nurse him. Keats's friend and confidant, Charles Armitage Brown, wrote, "Early one morning I was awakened in my bed by a pressure on my hand. It was Keats who came to tell me his brother was no more. I said nothing . . . at length, my thoughts returned from the dead to the living. I said 'Have nothing more to do with those lodgings—and alone too. Had you not better live with me?' He paused, pressed my hand warmly, and replied, 'I think it would be better.'"

Keats soon moved to Brown's house, which was called "Wentworth Place." Today it is better known as "Keats's House" (see Stop 28, below).

Cross Christchurch Hill and continue along Well Walk. At the iron fence, turn right, onto New End Square, to:

26. Burgh House, New End Square (tel. 071/431-0144), a fine Queen Anne home dating from 1703. The building was bought by Rev. Allatson Burgh in 1822, a minister who was accused of neglecting both his home and his congregation. Eventually the house came under control of the Burgh House Trust, which has established a small art museum here. The house is open Wednesday through Sunday from noon to 5pm.

Retrace your steps to Well Walk and continue straight ahead to Willow Road. Although it is a relatively long walk, the scenery here is beautiful since much of the route runs along Hampstead Heath. Take your third right to:

27. Downshire Hill, one of the most bucolic streets in Hampstead. Nearly all of the homes here are painstakingly preserved 19th-century structures.

Half a block to your right is:

FINAL REFUELING STOP   Freemasons Arms, 32 Downshire Hill (tel. 071/435-4498), a spacious tavern known for its good lunches and gaming spirit. This is one of the few remaining places in London where skittles is still played. Somewhat like American 10-pin bowling, skittles entails tossing a heavy wooden disk at nine pins placed 20 feet away. Games are held on Tuesday, Thursday, and Saturday nights, and the pub offers a trophy to the "best newcomer."

Exit the pub, walk 2 blocks down Downshire Hill, and turn left to Keats Grove. Three blocks ahead on your right is:

28. Keats's House (Wentworth Place), Keats Grove (tel. 071/435-2062), a rather unassuming home, where the Romantic poet John Keats (1795–1821) lived and worked. The poet, who was very fond of Hampstead, wrote:

> *To one who has been long in city pent,*
> *'Tis very sweet to look into the fair*
> *And open face of heaven.*

This well-preserved Regency house is now open to the public as a museum. It contains one of his first editions, as well as diaries, letters, assorted memorabilia, and some original furnishings. Keats's House is open April through October, Monday through Friday from 2 to 6pm, Saturday from 10am to 1pm and 2 to 5pm, and Sunday from 1 to 5pm. November through March it is open Monday through Friday and Sunday from 2 to 5pm, and Saturday from 10am to 1pm and 2 to 5pm.

APPENDIX

Recommended Reading

Hundreds, perhaps thousands, of books have been written about London, and thousands more about people who have lived there. We can read about the city through novels, plays, poems, histories, biographies, and guidebooks. Shakespeare and Dickens, two of Britain's best-known writers, exemplify those who can convey to us some idea of what London was like in earlier periods. We can also learn what everyday life was like and what concerned people through the works of such poets, playwrights, and novelists as William Blake, John Keats, Jane Austen, Emily and Charlotte Brontë, Lewis Carroll, George Eliot, and Oscar Wilde.

Virginia Woolf's *A Room of One's Own,* T.S. Eliot's *Wasteland,* and George Orwell's *Down and Out in Paris and London* are excellent literary windows into London's more recent past. London's social life is also evident in thousands of general-interest books, including some of the best mystery and suspense novels (for example, Sir Arthur Conan Doyle's Sherlock Holmes series and Agatha Christie's novels).

From an enormous number of books on and about London, we have chosen those that we believe represent the best.

Ackroyd, Peter, *Dickens' London: An Imaginative Vision* (Headline [UK] 1988).
    A selection of fictional and personal writings of one of London's greatest authors, which presents a detailed picture of the city in the early 19th century.

Clout, Hugh, *The Times London History Atlas* (HarperCollins, 1991).
    Street and regional maps, as well as historical information, from London's premier newspaper.

Doyle, Arthur Conan, *The Adventures and Memoirs of Sherlock Holmes* (Modern Library, 1946).
    A colorful, textured view of late 19th-century London, encompassing fiction's best-loved detective.

George, M. Dorothy, *London Life in the Eighteenth Century* (Academy Chicago Publishers, 1985).
    An enlightened and readable study of life in the Georgian period.

Graves, Robert, and Alan Hodge *Long Weekend: A Social History of Great Britain, 1918–1939* (Norton, 1963).
    A fascinating and straightforward account of Britain between the two World Wars.

Marshall, Dorothy, *Doctor Johnson's London* (Wiley, 1968).
    Marshall recreates the London that Dr. Johnson knew and loved, including its intellectual, literary, and artistic aspects.

Murrow, Edward R., *This Is London* (Schocken Books, 1989).
    London during World War II, as seen by the veteran CBS radio news reporter.

Pohl, Frederick Julius, *Like to the Lark: The Early Years of Shakespeare* (C. N. Potter, 1972).
    This book tries to reconstruct Shakespeare's "lost years" in London and answer many questions about his life.

Richards, Timothy M., *City of London Pubs: A Practical and Historical Guide* (Drake Publishers, 1973).
    The author guides visitors and history buffs through the many infamous pubs that have played a significant role in London's past.

Schwartz, Richard B., *Daily Life in Johnson's London* (University of Wisconsin Press, 1983).
    An acclaimed scholarly study of London—city and society— in the mid-18th century.

Trease, Geoffrey, *London: A Concise History* (Scribner's, 1975).
London's rich and varied past is examined from the heroic
days of the Blitz, through the city's second fire, to the period of
reconstruction that followed.

Waugh, Evelyn, *Brideshead Revisited* (Little, Brown, 1982).
Set partially in the home counties around the city and abroad,
this magnificent novel nonetheless describes to a tee London in
the early 20th century.

Weinreb, Ben, and Christopher Hibbert (eds.), *The London
Encyclopedia* (Adler & Adler, 1986).
The definitive source for in-depth information on thousands of
London buildings, institutions, and people.

Weintraub, Stanley, *The London Yankees: Portraits of American
Writers and Artists in England, 1894–1914* (Harcourt Brace,
1979).
Weintraub focuses on the politicking and private lives of
American authors and artists who spent considerable time in
London prior to World War I.

West, Paul, *The Women of Whitechapel and Jack the Ripper*
(Random House, 1991).
A fictional work that presents rich historical background
information, as well as actual facts, pertaining to the most
celebrated murder case in history.

Wilkes, John *The London Police in the Nineteenth Century*
(Lerner/Cambridge University Press, 1984).
The city, viewed from a unique perspective during its transi-
tion at the beginning of the Industrial Revolution.

Wilson, Jean M., *Virginia Woolf, Life and London: A Biography
of Place* (Norton, 1988).
Twentieth-century London is explored, with special attention
to the influence of the Bloomsbury circle of intellectuals and
artists.

ALSO WORTH THE READ

Barker, Felix, *London: 2,000 Years of a City and Its People*
(Macmillan, 1974).

Bennett, Arnold, *London Life* (Ayer, 1976).

Betjeman, John, *Victorian & Edwardian London* (David &
Charles, 1969).

Brewster, Dorothy, *Virginia Woolf's London* (Greenwood,
1979).

Brooke, Christopher, *London, 800–1216: The Shaping of a City* (Univ. of California Press, 1975).

Cameron, Robert, and Alistair Cooke, *Above London* (Cameron, 1980).

Defoe, Daniel, *Tour Thro' London About the Year 1725* (Ayer, 1929).

Ehrlich, Blake, *London on the Thames* (Little, Brown, 1966).

Ford, Ford Madox, *The Soul of London* (Haskell, 1972).

Goodard, Donald, *Blimey! Another Book About London* (Quadrangle Books, 1972).

Hibbert, Christopher *London: The Biography of a City* (Penguin, 1983).

James, Henry, *A London Life* (Arden, 1978).

Johnson, Samuel, *Johnson on Johnson: Personal Writings of Samuel Johnson* (Dutton, 1976).

Kirwan, Daniel J., *Palace and Hovel* (Abelard-Schuman, 1963).

Lejeune, Anthony, *The Gentlemen's Clubs of London* (Smith, 1979).

Olsen, Donald J., *The City As a Work of Art: London, Paris, Vienna* (Yale University Press, 1986).

Pepys, Samuel, *Everybody's Pepys: The Diary of Samuel Pepys 1660–1669* (Harcourt Brace, 1926).

Piper, David, *The Artist's London* (Oxford University Press, 1982).

Pritchett, Victor S., *London Perceived* (Harcourt Brace, 1966).

Swinnerton, Frank, *The Bookman's London* (R. West, 1980).

Thompson, John, *Orwell's London* (Schocken, 1985).

Timbs, John, *Clubs & Club Life in London with Anecdotes of Its Famous Coffee-Houses, Hostelries, & Taverns from the Seventeenth Century to the Present Time* (Gale, 1967).

Weightman, Gavin and Steve Humphries, *The Making of Modern London*.

Woolf, Virginia, *The London Scene* (Hallman, 1975).

Index

Please Send Me the Books Checked Below.

FROMMER'S COMPREHENSIVE GUIDES
(Guides listing facilities from budget to deluxe,
with emphasis on the medium-priced)

	Retail Price	Code		Retail Price	Code
☐ Acapulco/Ixtapa/Taxco 1993–94	$15.00	C120	☐ Jamaica/Barbados 1993–94	$15.00	C105
☐ Alaska 1990–91	$15.00	C001	☐ Japan 1992–93	$19.00	C020
☐ Arizona 1993–94	$18.00	C101	☐ Morocco 1992–93	$18.00	C021
☐ Australia 1992–93	$18.00	C002	☐ Nepal 1992–93	$18.00	C038
☐ Austria 1993–94	$19.00	C119	☐ New England 1993	$17.00	C114
☐ Austria/Hungary 1991–92	$15.00	C003	☐ New Mexico 1993–94	$15.00	C117
☐ Belgium/Holland/ Luxembourg 1993–94	$18.00	C106	☐ New York State 1992–93	$19.00	C025
☐ Bermuda/Bahamas 1992–93	$17.00	C005	☐ Northwest 1991–92	$17.00	C026
☐ Brazil 1993–94	$20.00	C111	☐ Portugal 1992–93	$16.00	C027
☐ California 1993	$18.00	C112	☐ Puerto Rico 1993–94	$15.00	C103
☐ Canada 1992–93	$18.00	C009	☐ Puerto Vallarta/ Manzanillo/Guadalajara 1992–93	$14.00	C028
☐ Caribbean 1993	$18.00	C102	☐ Scandinavia 1993–94	$19.00	C118
☐ Carolinas/Georgia 1992–93	$17.00	C034	☐ Scotland 1992–93	$16.00	C040
☐ Colorado 1993–94	$16.00	C100	☐ Skiing Europe 1989–90	$15.00	C030
☐ Cruises 1993–94	$19.00	C107	☐ South Pacific 1992–93	$20.00	C031
☐ DE/MD/PA & NJ Shore 1992–93	$19.00	C012	☐ Spain 1993–94	$19.00	C115
☐ Egypt 1990–91	$15.00	C013	☐ Switzerland/Liechtenstein 1992–93	$19.00	C032
☐ England 1993	$18.00	C109	☐ Thailand 1992–93	$20.00	C033
☐ Florida 1993	$18.00	C104	☐ U.S.A. 1993–94	$19.00	C116
☐ France 1992–93	$20.00	C017	☐ Virgin Islands 1992–93	$13.00	C036
☐ Germany 1993	$19.00	C108	☐ Virginia 1992–93	$14.00	C037
☐ Italy 1993	$19.00	C113	☐ Yucatan 1993–94	$18.00	C110

FROMMER'S $-A-DAY GUIDES
(Guides to low-cost tourist accommodations and facilities)

	Retail Price	Code		Retail Price	Code
☐ Australia on $45 1993–94	$18.00	D102	☐ Israel on $45 1993–94	$18.00	D101
☐ Costa Rica/Guatemala/ Belize on $35 1993–94	$17.00	D108	☐ Mexico on $50 1993	$19.00	D105
☐ Eastern Europe on $30 1993–94	$18.00	D110	☐ New York on $70 1992–93	$16.00	D016
☐ England on $60 1993	$18.00	D107	☐ New Zealand on $45 1993–94	$18.00	D103
☐ Europe on $45 1993	$19.00	D106	☐ Scotland/Wales on $50 1992–93	$18.00	D019
☐ Greece on $45 1993–94	$19.00	D100	☐ South America on $40 1993–94	$19.00	D109
☐ Hawaii on $75 1993	$19.00	D104	☐ Turkey on $40 1992–93	$22.00	D023
☐ India on $40 1992–93	$20.00	D010	☐ Washington, D.C. on $40 1992	$17.00	D024
☐ Ireland on $40 1992–93	$17.00	D011			

FROMMER'S CITY $-A-DAY GUIDES
(Pocket-size guides with an emphasis on low-cost tourist accommodations and facilities)

	Retail Price	Code		Retail Price	Code
☐ Berlin on $40 1992–93	$12.00	D002	☐ Madrid on $50 1992–93	$13.00	D014
☐ Copenhagen on $50 1992–93	$12.00	D003	☐ Paris on $45 1992–93	$12.00	D018
☐ London on $45 1992–93	$12.00	D013	☐ Stockholm on $50 1992–93	$13.00	D022

FROMMER'S WALKING TOURS
(With routes and detailed maps, these companion guides point out the places and pleasures that make a city unique)

	Retail Price	Code		Retail Price	Code
☐ Berlin	$12.00	W100	☐ Paris	$12.00	W103
☐ London	$12.00	W101	☐ San Francisco	$12.00	W104
☐ New York	$12.00	W102	☐ Washington, D.C.	$12.00	W105

FROMMER'S TOURING GUIDES
(Color-illustrated guides that include walking tours, cultural and historic sights, and practical information)

	Retail Price	Code		Retail Price	Code
☐ Amsterdam	$11.00	T001	☐ New York	$11.00	T008
☐ Barcelona	$14.00	T015	☐ Rome	$11.00	T010
☐ Brazil	$11.00	T003	☐ Scotland	$10.00	T011
☐ Florence	$ 9.00	T005	☐ Sicily	$15.00	T017
☐ Hong Kong/Singapore/			☐ Thailand	$13.00	T012
Macau	$11.00	T006	☐ Tokyo	$15.00	T016
☐ Kenya	$14.00	T018	☐ Venice	$ 9.00	T014
☐ London	$13.00	T007			

FROMMER'S FAMILY GUIDES

	Retail Price	Code		Retail Price	Code
☐ California with Kids	$18.00	F100	☐ San Francisco with Kids	$17.00	F004
☐ Los Angeles with Kids	$17.00	F002	☐ Washington, D.C. with		
☐ New York City with Kids	$18.00	F003	Kids	$17.00	F005

FROMMER'S CITY GUIDES
(Pocket-size guides to sightseeing and tourist accommodations and facilities in all price ranges)

	Retail Price	Code		Retail Price	Code
☐ Amsterdam 1993–94	$13.00	S110	☐ Miami 1993–94	$13.00	S118
☐ Athens 1993–94	$13.00	S114	☐ Minneapolis/St. Paul		
☐ Atlanta 1993–94	$13.00	S112	1993–94	$13.00	S119
☐ Atlantic City/Cape May			☐ Montreal/Quebec City		
1993–94	$13.00	S130	1993–94	$13.00	S125
☐ Bangkok 1992–93	$13.00	S005	☐ New Orleans 1993–94	$13.00	S103
☐ Barcelona/Majorca/			☐ New York 1993	$13.00	S120
Minorca/Ibiza 1993–94	$13.00	S115	☐ Orlando 1993	$13.00	S101
☐ Berlin 1993–94	$13.00	S116	☐ Paris 1993–94	$13.00	S109
☐ Boston 1993–94	$13.00	S117	☐ Philadelphia 1993–94	$13.00	S113
☐ Cancun/Cozumel/			☐ Rio 1991–92	$ 9.00	S029
Yucatan 1991–92	$ 9.00	S010	☐ Rome 1993–94	$13.00	S111
☐ Chicago 1993–94	$13.00	S122	☐ Salt Lake City 1991–92	$ 9.00	S031
☐ Denver/Boulder/			☐ San Diego 1993–94	$13.00	S107
Colorado Springs			☐ San Francisco 1993–94	$13.00	S104
1993–94	$13.00	S131	☐ Santa Fe/Taos/		
☐ Dublin 1993–94	$13.00	S128	Albuquerque 1993–94	$13.00	S108
☐ Hawaii 1992	$12.00	S014	☐ Seattle/Portland 1992–		
☐ Hong Kong 1992–93	$12.00	S015	93	$12.00	S035
☐ Honolulu/Oahu 1993	$13.00	S106	☐ St. Louis/Kansas City		
☐ Las Vegas 1993–94	$13.00	S121	1993–94	$13.00	S127
☐ Lisbon/Madrid/Costa			☐ Sydney 1993–94	$13.00	S129
del Sol 1991–92	$ 9.00	S017	☐ Tampa/St. Petersburg		
☐ London 1993	$13.00	S100	1993–94	$13.00	S105
☐ Los Angeles 1993–94	$13.00	S123	☐ Tokyo 1992–93	$13.00	S039
☐ Madrid/Costa del Sol			☐ Toronto 1993–94	$13.00	S126
1993–94	$13.00	S124	☐ Vancouver/Victoria		
☐ Mexico City/Acapulco			1990–91	$ 8.00	S041
1991–92	$ 9.00	S020	☐ Washington, D.C. 1993	$13.00	S102

Other Titles Available at Membership Prices
SPECIAL EDITIONS

	Retail Price	Code		Retail Price	Code
☐ Bed & Breakfast North America	$15.00	P002	☐ National Park Guide 1993	$15.00	P101
☐ Bed & Breakfast Southwest	$16.00	P100	☐ Where to Stay U.S.A.	$15.00	P102
☐ Caribbean Hideaways	$16.00	P005			
☐ Marilyn Wood's Wonderful Weekends (within a 250-mile radius of NYC)	$12.00	P017			

GAULT MILLAU'S "BEST OF" GUIDES
(The only guides that distinguish the truly superlative from the merely overrated)

	Retail Price	Code		Retail Price	Code
☐ Chicago	$16.00	G002	☐ New England	$16.00	G010
☐ Florida	$17.00	G003	☐ New Orleans	$17.00	G011
☐ France	$17.00	G004	☐ New York	$17.00	G012
☐ Germany	$18.00	G018	☐ Paris	$17.00	G013
☐ Hawaii	$17.00	G006	☐ San Francisco	$17.00	G014
☐ Hong Kong	$17.00	G007	☐ Thailand	$18.00	G019
☐ London	$17.00	G009	☐ Toronto	$17.00	G020
☐ Los Angeles	$17.00	G005	☐ Washington, D.C.	$17.00	G017

THE REAL GUIDES
(Opinionated, politically aware guides for youthful budget-minded travelers)

	Retail Price	Code		Retail Price	Code
☐ Able to Travel	$20.00	R112	☐ Italy	$18.00	R125
☐ Amsterdam	$13.00	R100	☐ Kenya	$12.95	R015
☐ Barcelona	$13.00	R101	☐ Mexico	$11.95	R016
☐ Belgium/Holland/ Luxembourg	$16.00	R031	☐ Morocco	$14.00	R017
☐ Berlin	$13.00	R123	☐ Nepal	$14.00	R018
☐ Brazil	$13.95	R003	☐ New York	$13.00	R019
☐ California & the West Coast	$17.00	R121	☐ Paris	$13.00	R020
☐ Canada	$15.00	R103	☐ Peru	$12.95	R021
☐ Czech and Slovak Republics	$15.00	R124	☐ Poland	$13.95	R022
☐ Egypt	$19.00	R105	☐ Portugal	$16.00	R126
☐ Europe	$18.00	R122	☐ Prague	$15.00	R113
☐ Florida	$14.00	R006	☐ San Francisco & the Bay Area	$11.95	R024
☐ France	$18.00	R106	☐ Scandinavia	$14.95	R025
☐ Germany	$18.00	R107	☐ Spain	$16.00	R026
☐ Greece	$18.00	R108	☐ Thailand	$17.00	R119
☐ Guatemala/Belize	$14.00	R010	☐ Tunisia	$17.00	R115
☐ Hong Kong/Macau	$11.95	R011	☐ Turkey	$13.95	R027
☐ Hungary	$14.95	R118	☐ U.S.A.	$18.00	R117
☐ Ireland	$17.00	R120	☐ Venice	$11.95	R028
			☐ Women Travel	$12.95	R029
			☐ Yugoslavia	$12.95	R030